# BLETCHLEY PARK
## BRAINTEASERS

# BLETCHLEY PARK
## BRAINTEASERS

### SINCLAIR McKAY

HEADLINE

First published in 2017
by HEADLINE PUBLISHING GROUP

6

Cataloguing in Publication Data is available from the British Library

Trade Paperback ISBN 978 1 4722 5260 9

Designed by Couper Street Type Co.
Printed and bound in Great Britain by Clays Ltd, St Ives PLC

Headline's policy is to use papers that are natural, renewable and recyclable products and
made from wood grown in sustainable forests. The logging and manufacturing processes are
expected to conform to the environmental regulations of the country of origin.

HEADLINE PUBLISHING GROUP
An Hachette UK Company
Carmelite House
50 Victoria Embankment
London EC4 0DZ

www.headline.co.uk
www.hachette.co.uk

To the Bletchley Park Trust, and all those who work at
Bletchley Park today, who have not only lovingly restored
one of the greatest landmarks of our time, but who also do
such brilliant work in teaching younger generations about
the astonishing achievements of the codebreakers.

# CONTENTS

# INTRODUCTION

Not everyone who worked at Bletchley Park was a genius on the level of mathematician Alan Turing. But every recruit had a luminously inquisitive mind.

And the thousands of super-bright young women and men pulled into the wartime codebreaking centre – from all walks of life, and with all sorts of different talents – did often share one particularly striking attribute.

They all had an unusual appetite and love for puzzles.

In a few straightforward cases, this was to do with a natural taste for complicated equations and rich linguistics. After all, there were so many exceptional intellects gathered at this top-secret country estate in Buckinghamshire that some Bletchley townsfolk – none the wiser – thought the place was a special government lunatic asylum.

But not everyone there was an intellectual, and nor was it all maths and modern languages. There was something else too: the people gathered there, from whatever background – ordinary or extraordinary – all shared the ability to examine a problem from lots of different angles. And more: they shared the ability to relish and enjoy that problem.

The truly astonishing thing was this: by day and by night, these codebreaking men and women grappled with decryption problems that could cause terrible stress and even breakdowns. Yet when off duty, they often sought relief from this stress by diving into yet more puzzles.

The aim of this book is to present a wide range of the sorts of brainteasers, problems and enigmas that were either used to recruit the codebreakers, or were used by the codebreakers as a means of relaxing escapism from the day job.

Whatever their speciality – be it esoteric probability theories, an immersive knowledge of Japanese, a taste for colourful riddles, or simply a fierce addiction to the daily *Times* and *Telegraph* crosswords – the Bletchley Park codebreakers were wonderfully emblematic of a puzzle-loving nation. This taste came to suffuse the very philosophy of the establishment. The codebreakers had to be more than sharp, for the challenges they were to face in their work were the ultimate puzzles, upon which the fate of the nation depended.

When blackout came to Britain after the declaration of war against Germany in September 1939, the Government Code and Cypher School at Bletchley – the codebreaking department that had relocated from St James's Park in London to this country estate midway between Oxford and Cambridge – immediately started looking for the brightest and the best.

The directors of Bletchley had already begun a systematic sweep of the universities throughout 1938 and they would later spread that net very much wider. They started by homing in on the young undergraduates in the mathematics departments. They wanted these students because they knew that they would be needed to fight the German encryption machine called Enigma that had been invented at the end of the First World War and was known to be used by the Nazis. It was an electric cipher machine that could theoretically produce 159 million million million combinations of letters.

But codebreaking was an art as well as a science, and it stretched back over the years, decades, centuries. As the draughty wooden huts that would house all the top-secret decryption activity were being built around the grounds of the Bletchley Park estate, the recruiters became cannier.

As well as seeking mathematicians, they also began looking for gifted young people with exceptional language skills: fluent German was naturally a great advantage. Indeed, as the war went on, candidates were needed who could master Japanese within the space of a few short weeks. So once again, the directors sent their scouts through the universities, making discreet enquiries.

Universities alone, however, could not provide all the recruits. Intelligence comes in all forms, not necessarily in mortarboards and black gowns. Before the war, Bletchley's directors had also put word out in aristocratic circles: throughout the 1930s, young women from the smarter families had often been sent out to Germany and Switzerland to finishing schools, where they acquired an ease with the languages of continental Europe.

And the net was to be thrown wider yet, for there were to be thousands of bright young female recruits – volunteers for the Women's Royal Naval Service, Women's Auxiliary Airforce and Auxiliary Territorial Service – ushered into this shadowy, secret world, in order to operate the technology of the future. These Wrens, hailing from all sorts of different educational backgrounds and from all over the country, were selected by means of an innocuous-looking question on their application forms. The question asked if the candidates enjoyed mental recreations in the form of cryptic crosswords, or similar.

If the answer to this was yes, there followed several discreet intelligence tests. After which the brightest of these young women would find themselves issued with a ticket for a train journey to a clandestine destination, having sworn to keep secret for the rest of their lives the details of the crucial codebreaking work that was about to consume them. They would go on to become experts in the wiring and the workings of technology so intensely secret that at first not even Britain's closest allies knew about it.

Along the way, other kinds of talented individuals were cherry-picked by the Bletchley recruiters too. Various poets were pulled in to the codebreaking efforts. Again, an affinity and ear for the infinite possibilities of language was the hook. Then there were the musicians. One of the most striking aspects of the Bletchley Park story is that a huge proportion of the young men and women gathered there had an amazing aptitude for music. There were endless concerts in and around Bletchley Park. Among the codebreakers were gifted pianists, violinists, sopranos and tenors. There were composers and conductors; artists who would go on to have extraordinary post-war careers. Something in the rhythms and structure of music clearly correlated to the discipline of codebreaking.

And codebreaking was a discipline as old as civilisation itself. Bletchley's decrypting predecessors in the inter-war and Great War years had also been drawn from varied fields. Some were experts at working with ancient hieroglyphs from tombs and faded papyrus fragments. These were people who could reconstruct long-dead languages and long-lost stories by breaking different sorts of codes: the symbols employed by the pharaohs, the extinct languages found on clay tablets in the deserts of Persia. If one could summon a vanished civilisation from a series of mysterious symbols, then it followed that one could equally reconstruct the encoded messages sent by German officers in the field.

Last but not least among the talented lateral thinkers of Bletchley Park were the chess champions – young men recruited directly through the chess grapevine. To excel at chess is to master the ability to hold a hundred abstract possibilities in one's head while trying to out-think one's opponent and divine their intentions, so it follows that chess players made formidably brilliant codebreakers. This went not merely for the whizz-kids of Bletchley Park, but their Soviet counterparts deep in Russia too.

So it is clear how Bletchley Park came to be seen by so many who worked there as a kind of university, for it fizzed with youthful intellectual and artistic energy. For every socially awkward mathematician, there was a hilariously confident debutante; for every owlish classicist, conversing in ancient Greek, there was a swing-music-loving Wren who would pass the time with the most ferociously fiendish crosswords. The puzzles to be found in these pages are the sorts of problems they would have taken to with gusto: some indeed were recruited with exactly the types of problems presented here.

The crossword is the most famous of the butterfly nets with which the Bletchley directors caught their geniuses, so we must of course start there, but there were other conundrums too – ranging from lateral thinking tests to problems involving invented mythical languages. We've included a range of these here so you can begin to work out what sort of codebreaker you might have been. There are also examples here of the sorts of tests facing secret interception operatives: Morse code problems, in which the slightest lapse in accuracy could mean the difference between life and death.

All in all, the different sorts of puzzles presented here – some from archives, some directly inspired by the tests and challenges faced by Bletchley Park's brightest – are not only intended to be entertainingly mind-boggling. They also show that the young women and men who helped shorten the Second World War by some two years had brains that could happily turn somersaults through all sorts of enigmas: from Egyptian symbolism to surreal Lewis Carroll-style logic problems that would involve looking at the world upside down.

The codebreakers loved these sorts of exercises. It is to be hoped that you will find them delightful and addictive too.

# CHAPTER ONE

# THE WORLD'S MOST FAMOUS CROSSWORD

Alan Turing – the father of modern computing, Bletchley Park's most famous codebreaker and one of the most extraordinary minds of the twentieth century – was absolutely hopeless at crosswords.

'Maurice and Francis Price arranged a party with a treasure hunt last Sunday,' wrote Turing in a letter in 1937 while he was at Princeton University in America. 'There were 13 clues of various kinds, cryptograms, anagrams and others completely obscure to me. It was all very ingenious, but I am not much use at them.'

A little later in the war, when Turing had been sent out from England to join US cryptographers in Washington, a colleague asked for his help in solving that day's cryptic teaser. Turing's response? 'That's one of those *Herald Tribune* cryptograms,' he said. 'I've never been able to do THOSE!'

So it is startling to think that if Turing had taken on the *Daily Telegraph*'s famous 1942 challenge to solve its cryptic crossword in twelve minutes or under, he would not have succeeded – and as a result, might have missed out on one of the more striking ways of being recruited to Bletchley Park.

This section of puzzles features not only that particularly significant *Telegraph* crossword, but also other wartime crosswords from *The Times* – for as we shall see, these puzzles were a crucial part of the fabric of Bletchley Park life.

The crossword printed in the *Daily Telegraph* on 13 January 1942 now has its place in history as a particularly British approach to seeking out the most supple wartime minds.

It had all started innocuously enough. In the latter stages of 1941, as the war in North Africa was unfolding, letter writers to the *Daily Telegraph* seemed concerned not so much with military gains, or with rationing, or with seeking out Fifth Columnist spies – but more with the quality of the daily crossword. Among the readers' letters were complaints that it had simply become too easy.

These letters first caught the attention of W. A. J. Gavin of The Eccentric Club, a venerable Mayfair dining society which aimed for a membership of original thinkers. Gavin thought it would be amusing to put up a prize for a special challenge. He got in touch with *Daily Telegraph* editor Arthur Watson, who was immediately taken with Gavin's idea for a £100 prize for anyone solving the daily crossword in under twelve minutes.

It was an amusing stunt in its own right, but the idea of it also caught the imagination of several key Whitehall figures.

A challenge was issued to the readers of the *Telegraph*. Those who accepted came to sit in a special area of the *Telegraph* newsroom, and on that chilly grey morning in January 1942, five people succeeded in correctly filling in the puzzle in the allotted time. Though the prize money was a substantial sum, a greater prize lay behind it. Because also witnessing the competition were figures from a shadowy sub-department of MI6.

One of the winners was a man called Stanley Sedgewick. Interviewed many years afterwards, he said: 'I received a letter marked "confidential" inviting me, as a consequence of taking part in the *Daily Telegraph* "Crossword Time Test" to make an appointment to see Colonel Nicholls of the General Staff who "would very much like to see you on a matter of national importance".'

Mr Sedgewick duly went along to Whitehall and so it was – having signed the Official Secrets Act – that he was recruited to the Bletchley Park operation. He was told, he said, that he had a sufficiently 'twisted brain' for the arduous work to appeal. (The other winners were approached and coaxed in a similar fashion.)

At this point it should be intriguing to find out if any one of us in this modern age also possesses a sufficiently 'twisted' brain to match that original twelve-minute feat. Can you beat the clock by completing the historic crossword on the following pages in the allotted time – and if so, might you have been one of the people finding yourself being quietly approached by the War Office and then being told to report to 'Station X', the code-name for Bletchley?

Crossword solving became a ritual for some of the codebreakers. Some favoured the *Telegraph*; others *The Times*. Among the fans of the latter was Hut 6 codebreaker Rolf Noskwith. Whenever he and fellow Bletchley-ite Sarah Norton were on the train out from London Euston to return to their duties in Buckinghamshire, they would share *The Times*'s crossword – one of them solving one half before then passing it over.

And one guaranteed source of tension in the wooden huts – quite separate from the crushing pressure to get codebreaking results – concerned who got to *The Times* first each day. There was a semi-agreement whereby the crossword was copied out, so that the one in the newspaper would be left pristine for whoever came next.

The idea that there was a direct link between the crossword craze and the codebreaker's mind had spread from across the Atlantic. The American equivalent of Bletchley Park during the war was an establishment called Arlington Hall in Virginia, not far from Washington DC. One of its recruits was a man who did not merely solve crosswords: he compiled them.

William Lutwiniak had been a serious cryptic crossword enthusiast since his early teens. His passion – and his talent for winning 'cryptogram' competitions – brought him to the attention of the authorities.

Just before America entered the war in 1941, Lutwiniak recalled, 'I got a communication from the Signal Intelligence Service, William Friedman, asking me if I'd be interested in signing up for the army extension courses on cryptography and cryptanalysis . . . It had been one of my fondest dreams to some day be a cryptanalyst as a profession,' he continued. 'It never occurred to me that it might actually happen, I didn't think there was any such place in the government.'

## TELEGRAPH
### JANUARY 13TH 1942

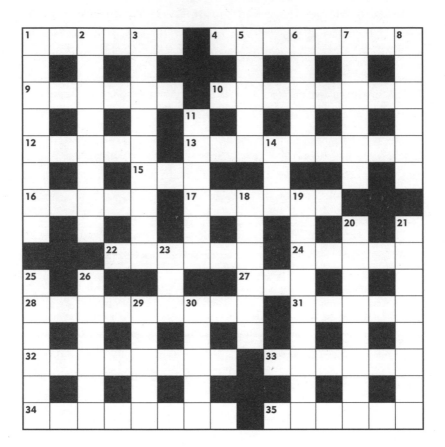

He ended up working for senior codebreaker Solomon Kullback, himself addicted to cryptic puzzles. After a spectacular secret cipher war focusing on German codes, Lutwiniak had the chance to pursue the career he really hankered for: devising cryptic newspaper crosswords full-time.

Britain's crosswords exerted a pull on American codebreakers too. Utah-born Frank W. Lewis had been inducted into cryptanalysis in his home country, and towards the end of the war he had been sent

## ACROSS

1. A stage company (6)
4. The direct route preferred by the Roundheads (5,3)
9. One of the ever-greens (6)
10. Scented (8)
12. Course with an apt finish (5)
13. Much that could be got from a timber merchant (5,4)
15. We have nothing and are in debt (3)
16. Pretend (5)
17. Is this town ready for a flood? (6)
22. The little fellow has some beer; it makes me lose colour, I say (6)
24. Fashion of a famous French family (5)
27. Tree (3)
28. One might of course use this tool to core an apple (6,3)
31. Once used for unofficial currency (5)
32. Those well brought up help these over stiles (4,4)
33. A sport in a hurry (6)
34. Is the workshop that turns out this part of a motor a hush-hush affair? (8)
35. An illumination functioning (6)

## DOWN

1. Official instruction not to forget the servants (8)
2. Said to be a remedy for a burn (5,3)
3. Kind of alias (9)
5. A disagreeable company (5)
6. Debtors may have to this money for their debts unless of course their creditors do it to the debts (5)
7. Boat that should be able to suit anyone (6)
8. Gear (6)
11. Business with the end in sight (6)
14. The right sort of woman to start a dame school (3)
18. 'The war' (anag.) (6)
19. When hammering take care not to hit this (5,4)
20. Making sound as a bell (8)
21. Half a fortnight of old (8)
23. Bird, dish or coin (3)
25. This sign of the Zodiac has no connection with the Fishes (6)
26. A preservative of teeth (6)
29. Famous sculptor (5)
30. This part of the locomotive engine would sound familiar to the golfer (5)

---

across the ocean to Bletchley Park. It was while he was there that he discovered the fabulous intricacies of the British cryptic crossword.

What started as an enthusiasm took over his (off-duty) life; when not attacking naval codes, Lewis immersed himself in all the tricks and stratagems employed by the cryptic crossword setters. Come the end of the war, this brilliant cryptanalyst returned to America and became a hugely respected figure in the top-secret National Security Agency. He imported those British crossword skills with him, becoming – like Lutwiniak – an enormously popular puzzle-setter. His chosen outlet was the *Nation* newspaper.

But that is not to say that Bletchley could not produce its own indigenous crossword compilers. Mathematician Shaun Wylie – who at university had side-stepped into classics, his extraordinary mind dancing across disciplines – was one of the most stalwart figures in Hut 8, working to demolish the German navy's codes, and later became a senior figure in the regenerated GCHQ. Perhaps tellingly, Wylie also gained an enormous amount of satisfaction compiling cryptic crosswords for *The Times* under the enigmatic pseudonym 'Petti'. These were said at the time to be the most fearsome puzzles set for a mainstream publication.

One Bletchley codebreaker, thinking back over his time at the Park some seventy-five years earlier, considered that breaking into Enigma codes required the sort of dual mind-set that was necessary for cryptic crosswords. He said that one had to be both ultra-focused and yet also relaxed, for no one had ever been able to solve a cryptic puzzle with a loaded gun pointed at their head.

Although cryptic crosswords during those war years were very similar to those enjoyed now, there is a suggestion that today's generation might struggle with the vintage puzzles. The linguistic double-backing and somersaulting is much the same but puzzlers then would also have been required to have a depth of general, cultural, classical and Biblical knowledge that might not necessarily be so prevalent now.

Phil McNeill, a recent puzzles editor of the *Daily Telegraph*, said of the crosswords that the newspaper printed in 1944 around D-Day: 'They were certainly more diverse. General knowledge clues nestled beside anagrams; riddles, or cryptic definitions, were to be found alongside quotations.

'Like today,' he continued, 'there were hidden words, homophones, double definitions and wordplay, but in a much looser format. It was a very mixed bag. I found it fascinating to try to think like a solver of the 1940s. Were they more literary than us? The compilers did like their poetic quotations. Were they better at lateral thinking? Some of these riddles certainly require a leap of the imagination. There are a few answers that you may never have come across.'

Added to this was one particular cultural consideration Mr McNeill faced when reprinting certain old puzzles: clues containing terms that would now be considered grossly offensive. 'There is one that we would not carry today as we are more sensitive – or less robust – about possible racial insults,' he said.

Old-fashioned terminology aside, both British and American codebreaking authorities understood very well how crossword puzzles might help the wider cryptological war effort, both in terms of sharpening methods of thinking, and also as a means of relaxing after a stressful shift.

They could also be used in more oblique ways: senior codebreaker Dilly Knox sometimes used puzzles as a metaphor to explain the work in hand to his new young recruits to Bletchley's 'Cottage' (a research department set up in a small house next to the stables). Incidentally, Knox's equally intelligent brother Ronald was a crossword show-off who once irritated Evelyn Waugh by solving all the 'across' answers of one cryptic puzzle, and then correctly filled in the 'down' answers without even looking at the clues.

So here is a fine selection of crosswords of a wartime vintage, selected from particularly auspicious days for Bletchley; days when vital codes were cracked, and when the Park was directly influencing the turning points of the war. These are the puzzles that codebreakers such as Stuart Milner-Barry were itching to solve even after the most gruelling, mind-shredding all-night shifts. The crosswords are presented here both as an enjoyable test and also as a means of gaining insight into the workings of the young minds that were solving them.

# 1

## *THE TIMES*

## AUGUST 15TH 1939

Several weeks before war is declared, the codebreaking operation moves from London to Bletchley.

## ACROSS

1. The speech of a baby elephant employs it, perhaps (11, 4)
9. Evidently I turn green with dizziness (7)
10. American inventor, not Oriental (7)
11. Indoor caps for the masses (4)
12. Not usually thought of as a composer of small beer (5)
13. She exhibits a miser's characteristic in 25 (4)
16. Section announcements (7)
17. The rarefied atmosphere necessary for vanishing tricks (4, 3)
18. The gardener is unfeeling with an inhabitant of his soil (7)
21. The mother insect is an elephantine creature (7)
23. Domesticated river (4) –
24. – and streams of fire-water? (5)
25. See 13 (4)
28. A freckle? (7)
29. It pulls a vehicle back on a hill (7)
30. Flag seen and felt unwillingly (5, 3, 7)

## DOWN

1. They have brought colour to our flags (two words) (8, 7)
2. Food that gets into the mouth of only a favoured horse? (7)
3. Chain letters? (4)
4. They seem foolish things to eat with soup (7)
5. '— as simplicity, and warm As ecstasy' (Cowper) (7)
6. A land where you are without a ship (4)
7. To fern may be sound, mother (7)
8. Ballet music is not their forte, however (5, 10)
14. Obsolete scuffle (5)
15. Diaphanous (5)
19. The country of the people in the song (7)
20. Where a relative is in not up (7)
21. Naturally they take some of the secretary's time (7)
22. Singular action popular among 8 (7)
26. How part of 4 can be taken (as it often is) musically! (4)
27 Just weather (4)

# 2

## THE TIMES

### JANUARY 2ND 1940

The first break into Enigma using the large perforated sheets of card known as 'Jeffrey sheets'.

## ACROSS

1. Poachers' wear? (9)
6. Tip or no tip (5)
9. They are very absorbing (5)
10. Not necessarily an inconsiderable period (9)
11. A swell affair (10)
12. An American girl can make it so different (4)
14. Ploughshare without puss (7)
15. Lordly wear (7)
17. Rests or places where you can get them (7)
19. Man to whom one doesn't mind lending (7)
20. It's in shocking taste (4)
22. Not articles of small arms (6, 4)
25. Queen Cole is evidently not at a loss for words (9)
26. Look for him in the Mile End Road (5)
27. Not a 'jam session' according to Carroll (5)
28. Hurry with the clue (9)

## DOWN

1. Dragged into matrimony? (5)
2. Adam couldn't claim them (9)
3. They progress without effort (10)
4. Retribution (7)
5. Not another name for dogfish (7)
6. Avuncular pledge (4)
7. His delight is play (5)
8. He takes great care (9)
13. Hyne's captain seems to enjoy good health in Yorkshire (10)
14. What dry rolls are probably made of (9)
16. The paint combine briefly? (9)
18. Ball for the angler (7)
19. Suitable nickname for the cup-holders (7)
21. Wordsworth's standard of loneli-ness (5)
23. This bread isn't (5)
24. A thing of custom (4)

# 3

## *THE TIMES*

## SEPTEMBER 2ND 1940

At the height of the Battle of Britain, Bletchley breaks into the Luftwaffe 'brown key' Enigma codes, helping air defence against the forthcoming Blitz.

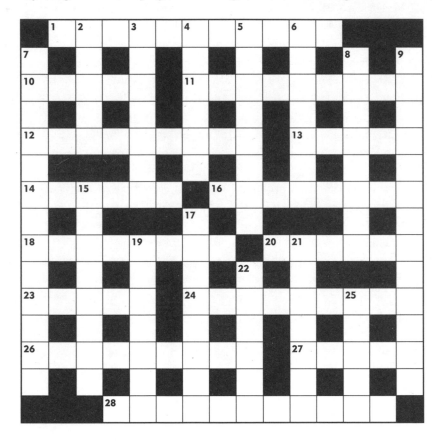

## ACROSS

1. Sir Robert Kindersley's idea of public virtue, perhaps (6, 5)
10. Bench wear (5)
11. High church abroad (9)
12. Having that sombre half holiday feeling? (9)
13. A little land having a tenant (5)
14. Assent (6)
16. One gets *The Times* back (8)
18. Description of Gilbert Jessop's idea of the way to score (3, 5)
20. Poster gone quick (6)
23. North-Western side (5)
24. Mob lawyer (anag.) (9)
26. It hardly suggests Dr. Gayda in a manner of speaking (5, 4)
27. Evidently the wood-worker is no fisherman (5)
28. Do these result from a correspondence course in journalism? (4, 7)

## DOWN

2. Announcement by the dog's victim (5)
3. Made secure (7)
4. 2 takes a letter for a ruse (6)
5. Rescued (8)
6. Goldsmith didn't make violoncellos (7)
7. It is not to imply that the flower in question sets a standard of impudence (5, 2, 1, 5)
8. Playgoers will remember Brewster's (8)
9. He has two arms, legs, wings and insides (6, 7)
15. Few people stay here long, however much they declare they like it (4, 4)
17. A Looking-glass day (8)
19. What Henry V was anxious should not be asked on St. Crispin's Day (3, 4)
21. Dance with the rest in confusion (7)
22. 'Thy Naiad airs have brought me home To the glory that was —' (Poe) (6)
25. She is not necessarily a matchmaker (5)

# 4

## *THE TIMES*

## MARCH 24TH 1941

The first of the crossword–puzzle–addicted Wrens arrive at Bletchley, there in part to operate the bombe code processing machines.

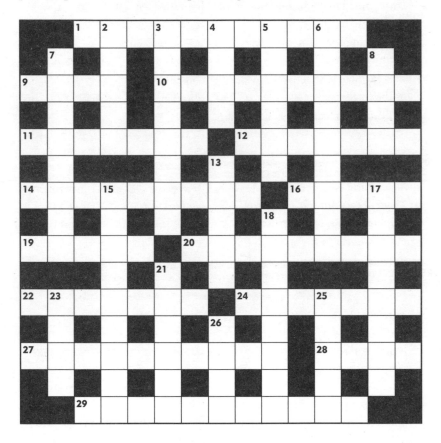

## ACROSS

1. Deportment in the strong-room? (4, 7)
9. A strapping sort of jumper (4).
10. Brainy (10)
11. This garment is for the protection of the kitchen front (7)
12. Bush-ranger's defeat? (7)
14. Apparently Oliver Twist wasn't (9)
16. Do they come into view in Lancashire? (5)
19. The cows are not sold to them (5)
20. She had many pressing suitors but found them all bores, so to speak (9)
22. What is she at? He supplies the answer (7)
24. The making of its first syllable – ask William of Wykeham (7)
27. Rides with mother having an outside attempt (10)
28. It may have sauce for a cargo (4)
29. A stethoscope will not discover if one is so (11)

## DOWN

2. It's simply all the rage (5)
3. But if they were one couldn't see whom to salute (4, 4)
4. Found in the repertoire of a concert party (4)
5. A bird with diver's interests (6)
6. This seems to be the place where the planning committee should meet (9)
7. Barry, I've made a book (8)
8. Bearing (4)
13. Hamlet referred to the law's (5)
15. It doesn't mean a man who falls down when skating (9)
17. Stuff produced from air and metal (8)
18. Heroic aspect of a broken musical instrument full of sand (8)
21. French hunting (6)
23. 'The cock's shrill clarion or the echoing —, No more shall rouse them from their lowly bed' (Gray) (4)
25. He seems the right man to have battled at Lord's (5)
26. The heathen, by implication, did (4)

# 5

## *THE TIMES*

## NOVEMBER 3RD 1942

As the desert war in North Africa turns, and The Battle of El Alamein is won, Bletchley has been working closely with its Cairo outstation, intercepting messages to German general Erwin Rommel, secretly contributing to the triumph.

## ACROSS

1. Terms of reference (7, 3, 5)
9. A journal 'in the know' should have many adherents (8)
10. Jews were not plagued here (6)
11. Novel treasure (6)
12. Drawn out, perhaps, and certainly awkward (8)
13. Something beefy is afoot (7)
15. MSS (7)
18. They keep themselves to themselves, as the saying goes (7)
19. Benedictine gratis (7)
21. Sound advice to a poseur? (1, 7)
24. Symbolic representation (6)
26. The company takes its rations back with it (6)
27. Evacuation, in their case, is made compulsory (8)
28. Good reading for the black-out (5, 10)

## DOWN

2. Suitable material of which to build a church? (9)
3. All's right with the world, she observed (5)
4. It will serve the purpose (9)
5. Not the Spitfire's cannon (6)
6. The first thing, as a rule, to do with an allotment (5)
7. One could make it with reels (9)
8. Four-footed guide (5)
14. It's candid, but seldom candied (4, 5)
16. Quite appropriate for the chips to come in with the fish (9)
17. For an up-to-date Daisy Bell, perhaps (3, 6)
20. The M.O. in the last state of confusion, or very near it (6)
22. Who goes there? I, O man! (5)
23. Drink up, as befits a king (5)
25. 'For frantic — and foolish word. Thy Mercyon Thy People, Lord' (Kipling) (5)

# 6

## *THE TIMES*

## JANUARY 18TH 1944

In conditions of top secrecy, the Colossus machine comes to Bletchley Park – a construction that can crack codes from Hitler himself and which also heralds the dawn of the computer age.

## ACROSS

1. I face blondes in Bucks (12)
9. A capital city (5)
10. Scarcely contains the whole of it (3)
11. A mess of game (5)
12. River of battle (4)
13. A means, perhaps, of confusing the issue (10)
15. Reeve, for example? (8)
17. 'The royal — and all quality, Pride, pomp and circumstance of glorious war' (*Othello*) (6)
20. To do so involves footwork (3)
22. His faith involves a change of 11 (6)
23. A festival to disregard (8)
25. This can be made with eight hands (10)
28. Jenny in uniform (4)
30. Room to move (5)
31. Sister and parent of a patriarch (3)
32. Sartorial geese (5)
33. Our dull-witted ancestors (6, 6)

## DOWN

2. Sand-eel if changed (9)
3., 14. A priestly vestment (8)
4. An orderly mob? (8)
5. Productive (6)
6. Sister of Lucie and Tillie (5)
7. High lama (5)
8. They are merely one's personal impressions (12)
9 . Unswervingly opposed, perhaps, to matrimony (12)
14. See 3
16. Unmanned hills (3)
18., 29. Bumptious (8)
19. The ultimate maximum? (9)
21. It is larger than the place in which it grows (8)
24. Limbs of a man of letters (6)
26. Shakespearian clown (5)
27. i.e., pull it (2, 3)
29. See 18

# 7

## *THE TIMES*

## JUNE 6TH 1944

D-Day – and as the Normandy landings are under way, the Bletchley code-breakers are decrypting all German communications and feeding the intelligence instantly to Winston Churchill.

## ACROSS

1. Some smart little beasts (9)
9. 'Go, lovely Rose' (—) (6)
10. Roman subsistence allowance (8)
11. It's a bore when they come into action (8)
13. Blessed in poetry (7)
14. The forty-ninth was dramatized (8)
15. Scoffs (5)
18. Part of 25 (3)
20. Cut down colour (3)
21. Genuinely attached to 28 (5)
24. Torturers did not add insult to injury by charging this up to their victims (8)
26. Snake in a coil (7)
27. Shot in the chest? (8)
29. A bonded store (8)
30. City mostly what a city inevitably is (6)
31. Sandy site for houses (9)

## DOWN

2. Anything but a steady movement (7)
3. The right place for anybody wanting a mattress? (7)
4. The saint is not in pain: quite the contrary, indeed (6)
5. 'E'en from the — the voice of nature cries' (Gray) (4)
6. Success in these depends largely on the use of one's hands (9)
7. Well, Nelly, the Minister of Food spells it differently (9)
8. Peel's Tory reconstruction (9)
12. Freshwater fish found in a salt-water ship (5)
15. Orestes was a legendary one (9)
16. It is only practised to deceive (9)
17. Rains cats (anag.) (9)
19. Apparent in the formation of Latin gerunds (5)
22. Account, perhaps, for the faked permits (7)
23. Fuel carrying on five (7)
25. Town wear (6)
28. It would be just after me (4)

# 8

## *THE TIMES*

## JULY 1ST 1944

Bletchley Park is now decoding more messages than ever before – some 4,500 communications a day – from theatres of war all around the world.

## ACROSS

1. J. Owl's impudence (5, 2, 4)
7. Singular gun dog (3)
9. There are whispers that we own the grog (7)
10. One means of putting shrews under (7)
11. Can you face it? (6)
12. Horatio, don't exclaim! (5)
15. Woman at the wheel. Not joy-riding, though (8)
16. Shell of somewhat milky appearance (6)
18. It demands elbow-room (6)
20. Tom's mare is quite a little creature (8)
23. I am hors-de-combat in the London suburb (5)
24. Vindictive when the French don't cheer (6)
27. Ran into Stevenson's Prince in Italy (7)
28. Final attachment (7)
29. In respect of which the Church cannot be accused of blindness (3)
30. Not a device for discovering if anybody has been at the decanter (11)

## DOWN

1. There is no credit in being sharper at this (4)
2. By Jane (4)
3. Not how you spell cow, young lady – unless it has gone to your head! (7)
4. Certainly, the soup dish was not intact last night (8)
5. They are taken, booked, worn and carried out (6)
6. Ran cool (anag.) (7)
7. The colour of its hair is always changing – for artistic effect (10)
8. The very flower of little operas! (10)
13. They are helpful to those who find it difficult to get up (10)
14. Land's End, Spain (10)
17. They seem to outlaw song (8)
19. These canaries never sing (7)
21. A saint, lace him (7)
22. Captured by Alexander's men (6)
25. Britons never will be what he just escapes being (4)
26. Singularly it is in the plural (4)

# 9

## *THE TIMES*

## MARCH 21ST 1945

Field Marshal Bernard Montgomery crosses the Rhine, helped in part by crystalline intelligence from Bletchley.

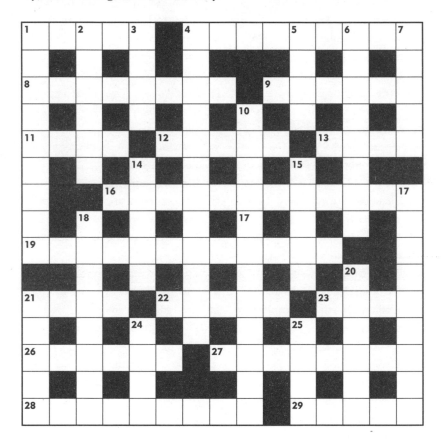

## ACROSS

1. It's a fake and that's where we get stuck (5)
4. A long time in the pantry (9)
8. Simply super if feline (8)
9. Its 8 are not quite so outstanding as those referred to in the clue (6)
11. I'm the unknown quantity, somewhat bucolic (4)
12. Cancel (5)
13. It often, when painful, gets black (4)
16. First cousin to a pedlar of dreams, perhaps (6, 6)
19. 'What a world of happiness,' sang Poe, 'their harmony foretells!' (7, 5)
21. Longing to be a batsman? (4)
22. It is found in the hosiery department (5)
23. A sheepish hero (4)
26. Dean of Barchester might end with a tent (6)
27. Where the addition is made is stated, though a suggestion of doubt follows (8)
28. He'd riches, and did this with them (9)
29. Awaited (5)

## DOWN

1. A little bit of India swallowed by a child's dog quite transparent (9)
2. Only half enough legging for 26 (6)
3. For this is deserting drink (4)
4. The right man to toast at a bump supper (12)
5. Greedy in a six-a-penny way (4)
6. Tut, and confuse the eagle (8)
7. Charlotte M. (5)
10. He dead might be the result of getting thus mentally disorganized (6, 6)
14. Little room here, afloat or ashore (5)
15. I am in the slot and capsized (5)
17. Claim in a musical instrument (9)
18. ' — , sans eyes, sans taste, sans everything,' so to speak (8)
20. Able and performed (6)
21. Foreign currency (5)
24. It's decreed, as it were (4)
25. She got her 'A' certificate, but didn't get . . . (4)

# 10

## *THE TIMES*

## MAY 8TH 1945

Victory in Europe – but apart from some drinks on the lawn and an address from the Bletchley vicar, the codebreaking work goes on, monitoring signals from the Far East and, a little later, from the Soviet Union.

## ACROSS

1. 'Nay, now you are too flat. And mar the concord with too harsh a —' (*Two G. of V.*) (7)
5. Miss Lee (7)
9. Fur coats I remodelled (9)
11. Part of Hamburg or Homburg (5)
12. Crime committed by an outsize female (6)
13. 'Here's flowers for you; Hot —, mints, savoury, marjoram' (*Winter's Tale*) (8)
15. Kipling people (4)
16. Is it a turning out of Tite Street ? (5, 5)
18. A Turk's cell is dim (10)
20. Puritan at a loss for a joke turns author (4)
23. Sumptuous quarters for a friend with a kinky tail (8)
24. Let it go hang (6)
26. He is simply revolting (5)
27. Fares to be revised (5, 4)
29. A limb of three feet (7)
30. He should be a good mixer (7)

## DOWN

1., 28. Not one who makes dough (6).
2. It takes the eye (7)
3. 'Close bosom-friend of the maturing sun' (Keats) (6)
4. Hardy soldier (4)
6. One might find him near Mons (8)
7. A wandering minstrel he (7)
8. Where the war-time controls are presumably not operative (7, 4)
10. It is, in a special sense, mine (8)
12. The drinks, on this occasion, are not 'on the house' (8)
14. The Scotsman manages to get the final tune (8)
17. 'Come you back to Mandalay Where the old — lay' (Kipling) (8)
19. One sort of bean (7)
21. Put me thus to be steamed (7)
22. One need not blush to wear it (6)
25. 'Pipe a song about a —' (Blake) (4)
28. See 1 down

CHAPTER TWO

# THE MORSE MASTERMINDS

For many decades, they were Bletchley Park's forgotten secret agents: thousands of young women and men, sitting in wooden (or bamboo) huts, in all manner of terrain from Cornwall to Cairo to Colombo, working around the clock to intercept all enemy radio messages – encrypted messages transmitted in Morse. This extraordinary global operation sent invaluable material back to the codebreakers, for the analysis that would enable them to see deep into battlefield plans and strategies.

The aim of the puzzles in this section is to give a flavour of the gruelling recruitment and training tests these young people faced. And also to give a sense of the unique toughness of this still largely unsung role: a glimpse into the mental agility of the secret listeners.

Some of these dedicated operatives would be listening in to pilots flying over the Channel; others would be carefully monitoring communications being sent around the Mediterranean. This was the raw material that was being fed back all day and all night to the cryptanalysts, and all of Bletchley's out-stations dotted around the country.

These recruits were working for the 'Y Service', the Y standing for 'wireless'. Like their codebreaking colleagues at Bletchley, they had all signed the Official Secrets Act; like those colleagues, they assumed that the penalty for giving away those secrets would be death. Their role was every bit as mind-wracking and pressurised as the work going on in the Bletchley huts. Most of their roles revolved around Morse: the dot-dot-dash code in which radio messages were transmitted. Very simply, sitting at their radio sets, they had to track down enemy transmissions, and then – with unerring accuracy and at extraordinary speed – transcribe and translate the Morse that was pouring through their headphones.

The ability to translate Morse accurately at speed was a skill learned with difficulty, one that required young, eager, elastic brains. To see and hear the dots and dashes, delivered incredibly quickly, and to instantly visualise the letters of the alphabet they signified, needed furious dedication and focus.

Like their Bletchley-based colleagues, the women and men of the Y Service arrived there having had their intelligence noted in aptitude tests. Pat Sinclair was a teenager from north London. In 1940, from the heights of her hilly suburb, she had seen first-hand the horror of the Blitz. This made her utterly determined to sign up to do her bit.

While working for the local electricity board, Pat taught herself Morse code, with the help of a radio enthusiast friend. Her aim was to get into the Wrens – firstly because she was attracted to the possibility of this sort of intelligence work, and secondly because she regarded it as the most glamorous of the services.

Her gambit worked: she told the recruiters she could manage five words a minute in Morse so she was duly packed off to a camp in the suburb of Mill Hill to take a wireless telegraphy course. She was swiftly to discover that the intensity of the work could create casualties.

This was also found by fellow young Londoner Bob Roberts, from Islington, who had gravitated towards this branch of code-work because of his overwhelming love and obsession for the technology of radio. He was sent to Skegness for training; like Pat Sinclair, he quickly discovered what was required. These Y Service whizz-kids – soon to prove completely invaluable to the Bletchley operation – would be asked to reel off twenty to thirty words a minute from Morse; this was a breathtaking proposition, requiring superhuman speed of thought and reaction.

Clearly not everyone could do it. Bob Roberts remembered how even in the early stages of training, the pressure became too much for some recruits, who were forced to withdraw after suffering mini-breakdowns. Adding to the difficulty was the knowledge that total accuracy was required; anything less and lives on the battlefield would be lost.

More pressure was to come. While some recruits would be based in stations dotted around Britain – from the wilds of Wick in Scotland to huts not far from the white cliffs of Dover – many other young women and men would find themselves boarding ships to destinations unknown.

Some Wrens found themselves posted to Egypt – a Bletchley codebreaking outpost in Cairo – working amid vivid colours, intoxicating scents and all-pervasive sand. Others were dispatched further yet, to Colombo in Ceylon, where they would find themselves intercepting Japanese coded messages in huts with ceiling fans and regular invasions from snakes and insects.

Among the men, Bob Roberts was posted to Alexandria, Egypt, faced with a new world of heat, blinding sun on white dunes, and flies. He secretly intercepted enemy messages through the night: sometimes there were desert thunderstorms which – if you did not grab the headphones off fast enough – could cause permanent hearing problems as the roar of the thunder came shooting down the wires.

Then there was Peter Budd, a teenager from Bristol, who found himself on the other side of the world in an unspoiled paradise: a secret listener in the Cocos Islands deep in the Indian Ocean. To counter the pressure and intensity of the work monitoring Japanese vessels and aeroplanes, he and his colleagues were lucky enough to find themselves in a rich realm of emerald foliage and pale blue waters, with plentiful supplies of fruit, beer and gramophone records.

The linking factor between all these men and women was the amazing elasticity of their brains. Not only did they relish puzzles, but they also had the capacity to work at high speed: not merely instantly translating Morse but also dealing with the multiple distractions – fuzzy frequencies, competing voices – that could potentially cause confusion.

It also became clear that age was a crucial factor. Secret listeners over the age of thirty would often find the work trickier; indeed, the stress led to some being taken away for medical attention.

It was a while before Wren Anne Glyn-Jones – training in rural Devon in 1942 – was let in on the secret of why she was being drilled in Morse to this level of intensity. But she soon found herself being posted to Gibraltar, a particular hotspot during the war, as well as a crucial Bletchley/Y Service out-station. She wrote: 'Every day we ditted and dahed. Visualising Morse as a series of dots and dashes was rapidly eliminated from our minds; speed depended on our capacity to achieve a completely automatic connection between what we heard and what we wrote down.

'The connection between ear and hand had become so automatic that we ceased to use the conscious part of our minds,' she added. 'I remember a moment of panic when I completely forgot what the symbol "dit-dah" meant, and while I struggled to remember, I watched with interest as my own hand reacted to the stimulus by writing – quite correctly – the letter "A".'

Morse now is almost extinct: it was killed off by the advent of the digital age. (That said, there are sailors and pilots who still sensibly take the precaution of learning it in case of general computer breakdown.) By and large it is difficult now to imagine just how skilled the secret listeners were. They not only became proficient in a language that appeared to the uninitiated as merely a series of beeps, but in a curious way they also got to know the various enemy Morse operators who were sending the messages.

The secret listeners came to recognise what they called 'fists'; that is, the operating style of those who were sending the messages. Many said that somehow, they came to know a little of their counterparts' personalities as a result.

Ray Fawcett was one such secret listener who recalled that there was almost a curious intimacy between the interceptors and the people sending the messages out. Those Germans knew that their communications were being harvested – because they were of course in turn harvesting British messages.

Even more directly, there were Wrens engaged in interception on the south coast of England – installed in little wooden huts, exposed to German fighter fire while listening to the messages passing between the Luftwaffe pilots.

The pilots knew that young women were eavesdropping on them; sometimes they called out jokey, suggestive phrases in English to let the Wrens know. Some Wren veterans later said that they came to feel a little fond of these young German men, and always felt curiously stricken when they were shot out of the sky by defending British pilots.

At the core of all this was the fact that Y Service operatives prided themselves on a certain mental agility. For Pat Sinclair, learning this new technical skill was, she recalled, a little like shorthand, only much more complex and with rather graver consequences if any mistakes were made. Based in the Nissen huts at HMS Flowerdown, near Winchester, Hampshire, she worked exhausting shifts deep into the night, supervisors taking all the Morse that she had transcribed on special sheets, and sending these letters off for decryption at Bletchley Park.

And for these women and men alike, there was curiosity too about the science of radio transmission: the way that signals would bounce off the ionosphere, the means by which one could focus one's interceptions on enemies many miles away. As a result, these operatives were perhaps slightly more practical-minded than some of the boffins at Bletchley Park; these were people who could disassemble and reconstruct complex radio sets without a second thought. The training they received was also about developing a certain level of mental toughness. The tests they faced almost turned their brains into computers.

The time element was obviously vital too: in the flames of battle, when orders and messages were flying to and fro with lightning speed, the secret interceptors had to be focused to an almost preternatural degree. Imagine then that pressure when one was stationed deep in the heart of a sweltering jungle, or (as in the case of Bob Roberts in a later posting) high up in a mountain hut in the dead of night in southern Italy – with the place suddenly surrounded by hungry mountain dogs.

The puzzles in this section are in part intended as a tribute to these neglected listeners: a series of Morse messages, with keys, but with the proviso that the messages must be translated and decoded against increasingly tight time limits. Though it is obviously impossible to replicate the searing pressure that the secret operatives worked under, the puzzles might just give an insight into the sort of challenges they would have faced.

*For some of these puzzles, you will need to know the Morse symbols, as found in the following table:*

### MORSE SYMBOLS

#### Alphabet

| | | | | | | | | | |
|---|---|---|---|---|---|---|---|---|---|
| A | • – | G | – – • | M | – – | S | • • • | Y | – • – – |
| B | – • • • | H | • • • • | N | – • | T | – | Z | – – • • |
| C | – • – • | I | • • | O | – – – | U | • • – | | |
| D | – • • | J | • – – – | P | • – – • | V | • • • – | | |
| E | • | K | – • – | Q | – – • – | W | • – – | | |
| F | • • – • | L | • – • • | R | • – • | X | – • • – | | |

#### Numerals

| | | | | | | | | | |
|---|---|---|---|---|---|---|---|---|---|
| 1 | • – – – – | 3 | • • • – – | 5 | • • • • • | 7 | – – • • • | 9 | – – – – • |
| 2 | • • – – – | 4 | • • • • – | 6 | – • • • • | 8 | – – – • • | 0 | – – – – – |

# 1

## THE FIRST MORSE MESSAGE

On 24 May 1844, almost a hundred years before World War II, Samuel Morse sent his first Morse code message using a dot and dash code, between Washington and Baltimore. It was sent by means of sound down a telegraph wire and his very first message was: 'WHAT HATH GOD WROUGHT.'

Decipher the message below which uses the same letters as Morse did all those years ago in that original communication – but not in the same order! A / signals the end of a word. You have 5 minutes to complete this assignment.

– – –  • • –  – – •  • • • •  – / –  – – – / – • •  – – – /
– – •  – – –  – – –  – • • /

–  • • • •  • – •  – – –  • • –  – – •  • • • •  – – –  • • –  – /
–  • • • •  • –  – / • – –  • –  • – • .

# 2
## DISASTER TRANSMISSION

A message received at Bletchley towards the end of World War II. Can you decipher the message, including the month of its transmission? You have 6 minutes to finish.

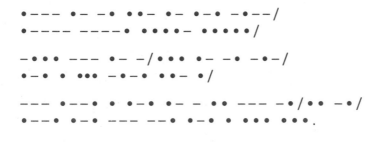

# 3
## KEYBOARD CRISIS

A Morse code message has been decoded by the boffins across the Park and the message must go now! Unfortunately the typewriter has seized up and only the top line of the qwerty typewriter is functional. So for example, the number 6 could be a Y, an H or an N. Remember also a number might be just that – a number.

By pressing the number keys a choice of letters is possible but with speed, accuracy and logical deduction can you work out the correct message?

**a)** 8 7 7 8 6 3 6 5 / 3 3 0 1 4 5 7 4 3 / 5 3 / 0 4 3 0 1 4 3 3 / 5 9 / 1 7 8 5 / 2 1 4 3 / 6 9 7 2 3 / 2 8 5 6 9 7 5 / 3 3 9 1 6.

But it's not always bad news . . .

**b)** 0 3 6 3 9 9 0 3 / 1 4 4 8 4 3 2 / 0 9 4 5 2 7 9 7 5 6 / 4 0 7!

# 4
## OVER TO YOU

Try your hand at translating this message into Morse code. It is taken from an authentic message transmitted in 1944. You have 6 minutes to complete the translation accurately.

ARROMANCHES UNDER FIRE. REINFORCED AIR RECCE.
JUNE 6 NORMANDY.

# 5
## HEARTBEAT

**a)** Julius Caesar recorded the square root of 25, and linked it via Morse code to a piece of classical music.

**b)** The recording of two vowels might tell you to 'put that light out', however old you were.

**c)** And why might 9T make everyone stand up?

# 6
## MORALE BOOSTER

A message from May 1941, intercepted by Bletchley, highlighting the need to keep the propaganda war alive. You have 9 minutes to decipher the message.

– – – – / – • – • – – – – – – – • – – • – • • • • • – • /
• • – • / – • – • • • • • • • • • • – • /

• – • • – • • – • • – – – • – – / • • / – • • • • • – – • – • – /
– • – – – – – • • – / • • – • /

– • • • • • / – • • – – – • / – – – • • – • / – • • • • • /
• – • – • • • – • • /

– – • • • – • – – – • – – • / • – – • • – – – • – – • • – • • • /
• – – • • – – – • – • • • • – • / • • • • • • – • – • • • • – • .

# 7
## DASH IT ALL, DOT!

What is the link in the listed words below?

**a)** T E E

**b)** M A I N

**c)** W O R K S

**d)** F L Y

**e)** And if you've dashed off the solutions to those, what about S H E and T O M?

# 8
## UNDER PRESSURE

Over to you again to send out the message. Lives depend on it. Speed and accuracy are of the essence. You have 5 minutes from the time you start. You should be getting quicker at this now so the time allotted per word is getting shorter!

FROM U1103 EISELE TO CAPTAIN U BOAT BALTIC. TUBE NUMBER 4 LEAKING, FLOODING AND DRAINING.

# 9
## BLITZ

Each numbered line of Morse code letters can be split into two names of places of the same length when decoded. Unfortunately the lines have been scrambled but the names still read from left to right, and are in the correct sequence. Translate the Morse code and work out the names in question. You have 12 minutes to complete this task.

1   •——  ••  •—  —  •—  •——•  •—••  •—  —•——  —•

2   ——  •—•  •—  ••••  ••  •—••  —  •—  —•  •

3   •——•  —••  •—  ———  •—•  •••—  ••  •••  •  •—•

4   •—••  •——  ———  •—  •—•  —•  —••  •••  •—  •——
     ———  —•

5   —•••  •  ——  ———  •—•  •••  —•—•  •—••  ———
     •——  ••  —•

# 10

## SWITCHBOARD

Everyone played their part at Bletchley Park. Telephone systems relied on alert operators being able to make sure that all communications were properly routed.

Starting with the letter given in the bottom left-hand corner of the grid opposite, make the connections to link all the listed words back up the grid to form a chain in which words overlap (words may read backwards or forwards depending on the direction of the arrows). The last letter of each word is also the first of the next. When a word *finishes* in a numbered square move straight to the other square in the grid that contains the same number. Repeat the last letter, then continue. Take care! There are many permutations but only one complete answer.

| | | | | | | |
|---|---|---|---|---|---|---|
| ARMADA | CIRCUS | DIRECT | DYNAMO | ENDING | FINISH | GALLOP |
| HALVES | KNIGHT | LINTEL | LIQUID | MOSAIC | NEBULA | NORMAL |
| OPTION | POTION | RECTOR | RETORT | SQUEAK | SYSTEM | TARIFF |
| TEAPOT | TEMPLE | TORRID | TURRET | YONDER | | |

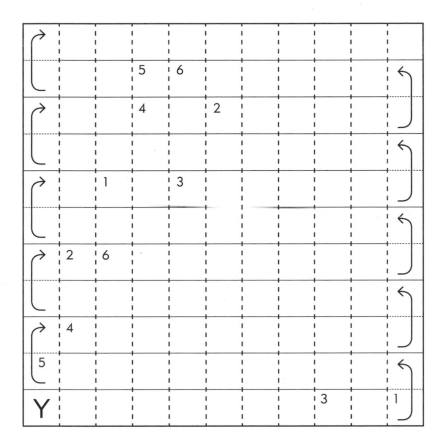

# CHAPTER THREE

# THE ENIGMA CONNECTIONS

At first glance, the Enigma machine – a beguiling marvel of Bakelite and brass – seems almost to have been designed to appeal to puzzle enthusiasts. There is a delicious, illusory simplicity about the look of the thing; yet for all those recruited to Bletchley Park to penetrate to the heart of its awesome capabilities, that illusion was very quickly dissolved.

The Enigma machine was revolutionary, but actually, the principle that it worked on was as old as the centuries. Despite the technological sophistication, it was still all about substituting one letter for another. The encryption puzzles in this section are intended to reflect the patient discipline that Bletchley codebreakers had to acquire. Especially when facing the prospect of diving into a vortex of chaos.

Enigma was the twentieth-century culmination of 2,000 years of cunning. There have been secret ciphers as long as there have been empires and writing. In Roman times, the 'Caesar Shift' – an encoding technique named after the emperor – allowed generals to communicate by means of transposition. Each letter would be encoded by means of an agreed formula, such as A becoming D, B becoming E, C becoming F – all moved three letters along.

Methods naturally grew more complex. By the time of Tudor England, for instance, Henry VIII's secretary Thomas More was using sophisticated ciphers in his letters to Cardinal Wolsey; some decades later, intercepted Catholic codes proved the downfall of Elizabeth I's enemy Mary Queen of Scots.

The Elizabethan spymaster Sir Francis Walsingham was said to have been an enthusiast for 'trellis' ciphers. The trellis technique was especially nifty. The agent in the field would have in his possession a secret document that, if captured, would simply look like many lines of apparently random letters. There would be no sense of words, or phrases, or sentences in the midst of that chaos.

It could only be unlocked by the recipient with what was termed a 'trellis', a length of blank parchment with eight to twelve holes dotted in it, with no apparent pattern.

When this 'trellis' was laid down upon the encoded document, the holes revealed the individual letters beneath. These letters would normally add up to a single word or name of significance.

Obviously, the system had its limits, and relied upon a great deal of foreknowledge on either side of the communication. Nonetheless, as a quick and easy means – for example – of dictating where a trusted agent was heading for next, it proved popular.

Elsewhere, in continental Europe, where religious war had been roaring throughout the late medieval period, even more sophisticated ciphers were needed. In sixteenth-century France, the Vigenère Square – a 26-by-26-square grid, filled with the letters of the alphabet shifted along once in each row – was the means by which kings and merchants began to conduct their careful confidential affairs.

This ingenious new system had been named after the diplomat Blaise de Vigènere. The principle at least was very simple. While letter substitution – A becomes C, etc. – was speedy, it was also very easy to crack. It didn't take much to carefully check the frequency of letters in a coded message: if 'K' turned up a disproportionate number of times in the code, then any cryptographer might fathom that 'K' was the substitute for the common letters 'E' or 'A'.

So a more effective way to scramble a message would be to use not just one but multiple different sets of alphabets. These could all be placed neatly into a square, each set of letters shifted along one place in each different row.

Say the message to be encrypted was: 'SOLVE THIS PUZZLE'. You would then choose a keyword, say 'ENIGMA'. So to turn 'SOLVE

THIS PUZZLE' into code, under those letters you would write out 'ENIGMA' repeatedly thus:

SOLVETHISPUZZLE

ENIGMAENIGMAENI

This done, you would turn to your Vigènere Square of letters. The first letter of the message would be matched with the first letter of the keyword, so you would track along the first row to S, and check down the vertical column to E. The letter at the intersection would provide the code letter. The procedure would be repeated for all the other letters in the phrase. The resulting series of letters would be completely unintelligible without the keyword to unlock it.

It sounds cumbersome when described but was actually swift and easy to use. And another advantage of this system was its sheer pleasing elegance: a simple square of letters on a piece of vellum. Indeed, the system was considered so effective that for the space of some 300 years or so, there were many who considered it unbreakable – though it is said that partway through the nineteenth century, the great thinker (and pioneer of computing philosophy) Charles Babbage, working in London, was thought to have found a way into the code without ever needing to know what keyword was being used to lock it.

By the mid-1850s, with the British seizing ever more colonial territory around the world, Charles Wheatstone devised an even more layered coding system that was so effective that it was still being used by British and Germans alike in the early years of the Second World War. It became known as 'Playfair' or 'The Playfair Cipher' because its use had been widely popularised by Lord Playfair.

Again, the appeal of it was its superficial ease of use. It consisted of another square filled with letters – but far fewer than the great mass to be seen in Vigènere's Square. The difference this time was that it was not single letters that were substituted but pairs of letters. The reasoning was that even in the complex codes, exhaustive frequency analysis – looking for those 'E's and 'A's – would eventually unravel the cipher.

With Playfair, the paired letters meant that the mathematical odds were multiplied many more times. An entire department of codebreakers could conceivably spend months exhaustively trying out all sorts of different combinations before they found the key.

Or at least so the redoubtable Lord Playfair might have thought when he popularised it in the nineteenth century. By the time the technique had spread, and the Nazis were using it in the field for low-grade messages (Playfair didn't need machinery – just pencil and paper with the keywords to set it up – which meant it was very good for instant short-range, fast communication on the battlefield), the whizzkids at Bletchley Park had found a way in.

No matter that most of their time was devoted to Enigma and later electronic variants: deciphering Playfair was almost a point of pride. Captain Jerry Roberts was among the young men pulled away from active duty in the early 1940s to lend their brainpower to the coding efforts. Studying Playfair was his initiation into the deeper complexities of modern coding systems. Another young recruit pulled in from the army called Roy Jenkins found that Playfair was altogether quite a slog; his later role as Home Secretary in the 1960s government of Harold Wilson was rather easier-going on the brain cells.

But that was the thing. None of the code-formulating techniques mentioned here belonged to the mechanised age. No matter how brilliant and mathematically difficult to pierce all these ciphers were, they were always formulated with the human touch: devised by the human mind and always unravelled by human hand.

This had remained the case all the way through to the First World War. In its immediate aftermath, however, a fresh revolution occurred. It might be termed the Industrial Cipher Revolution.

In the aftermath of the Great War, a German businessman called Arthur Scherbius – navigating the tumultuous tides of the Weimar Republic, with its post-war trauma and economic calamity – had been brooding about keeping business secrets completely secure.

The problem with human-made codes was that it was always only a matter of time before human ingenuity could unravel them.

The new possibilities opened up by electricity – and indeed the coming of the typewriter – led Scherbius to develop his first encryption machine on the models that soon followed. A letter pressed on the keyboard would cause a bakelite rotor to move and in turn light up a corresponding encoded letter on a lampboard above.

There were three rotors, each with all twenty-six letters. To generate a code, they would be fitted into the machine's slots in agreed positions. Once the machine had generated the encoded letters, the message could be sent in Morse or by telegraph.

The operator at the other end – his own machine set up with the rotors in identical positions – would type the coded letters on to the keyboard. The letters that then lit up on the board above were the uncoded ones. The message could thus be pieced together.

When Scherbius patented his machine, which he called Enigma, the original intention was that it should be aimed at banks and insurance companies. In the wake of the Great War, it was not going to be used for German military applications.

But by 1926, that changed. The technology – which had been through several evolutionary changes – was looked at by the German Navy. It was also studied by the British military. The latter turned it down. The German Navy adopted it.

In the years that followed, its use spread to all the German military services, as they became beholden to the newly triumphant Nazi party.

Mussolini's Italian fascists picked up on their own version of Enigma too. The attraction was obvious. It was a superbly portable code-generating machine that came in an easy-to-carry box, and it could be used anywhere, from the howling sands of the desert, to the black depths of the ocean in a submarine.

A machine that could generate a potential 159 million million million different codes. Not one of its users ever imagined that the human mind could find a lever into it. What human could match this electric marvel?

Well, one such man was Alfred Dillwyn Knox, known affectionately as 'Dilly'. A mainstay of the Admiralty's codebreaking department Room 40 during the First World War, he had stayed on throughout the 1920s and 1930s with what became the Government Code and Cypher School. He was intrigued by the fiendish challenge posed by the Enigma. He knew that when the German military acquired it, they would modify it to tighten its security further. A classicist by training – steeped in ancient Latin and Greek – Knox had a mind that could work in multiple dimensions simultaneously. And he believed that despite the electric complexities, there must be some tiny flaw in the logical structure of the Enigma that would enable codebreakers to jemmy their way in.

He was not alone. In 1930s Poland – unhappily pressed between the rising Nazis and Stalin, Russia's 'man of steel' – three brilliant mathematicians, led by Marian Rejewski, were also pondering the labyrinthine complications of Enigma. In the late 1930s, they were the first to devise methods to cast a chink of light into the device's inner workings. One such method was named after the mathematician Henryk Zygalski. The Zygalski sheets – resembling gigantic punch-cards with strategically placed holes – was a dazzlingly abstruse idea that involved shining lights through successive sheets with successive combinations of letters matching possible Enigma settings until the light only shone through one hole.

Another method was to fight electrics with electrics: this involved an invention they called the bomba machine, named not after explosives, but after the 'bomba' ice-cream dessert. This hulking machine involved rotating drums, with letters upon them. If given certain combinations of letters, this machine could chew its way through many more permutations than any human.

In July 1939, just weeks before Hitler's forces brutally smashed through Poland, the mathematicians met with Dilly Knox and several other key Bletchley personnel in a dark forest outside Warsaw. They passed this invaluable baton of knowledge on.

Back at Bletchley, the Polish methods were adapted and developed: Zygalski's ingenious process involving the hole-punched sheets of card, and Alan Turing and Gordon Welchman, together with engineer Harold Keen, got on the case.

Alan Turing – just twenty-seven years old when he started at Bletchley, his name having been on a list since 1938 – had already made an academic name for himself at Cambridge and Princeton with his revolutionary paper 'On Computable Numbers'. Gordon Welchman, then thirty-three, and a former Cambridge maths lecturer with an unusually dashing matinee idol style, had been headhunted early. He fast became the organisational genius of Bletchley, sorting out the focus of each different codebreaking department.

Together with Keene, Turing and Welchman summoned forth a mechanical marvel which they called the bombe machine. It was the size of a wardrobe, filled with spinning drums that could devour its way through 17,576 code combination possibilities in the fraction of the time it would take a human to do so.

As the war progressed, hundreds of these machines were built – and they in turn were followed by the Colossus, which was essentially the world's first computer. This was the technology that would shape the future – and it needed operators with lightning-fast minds.

The young undergraduates being recruited to Bletchley in the early years of the war obviously had never heard about – still yet seen – the Enigma. There was but one captured machine at the Park. Keith Batey remembered that when he arrived as a twenty-year-old at Hut 6, he was given a brief induction that basically involved a quick examination of the machine and its wiring.

He observed the keyboard, the lampboard, the rotors and the new level of security – what was called the 'steckerboard', a maze of electric wires that directed the current along a different path when moving the letter rotors.

And that was it. Mr Batey was required to move from that to conceiving of weaknesses that could render this fearsome proposition vulnerable.

There was one tiny weakness in the Enigma, which had first been observed by Marian Rejewski and Dilly Knox: a trifling thing that on first sight might have had no significance. Despite all the millions and millions of combinations, the Enigma would never encode a letter as itself. For example, if you typed 'A', the coded letter which lit up above would never be an 'A'.

This might not have sounded very promising but such a quality left open the tantalising possibility that some higher mathematical method could be devised to use it as a crowbar. But Knox sensed that this feature might produce observable bumps or glitches if sufficiently huge quantities of encoded material were gathered.

With the help of the Turing bombe machines – which could chew through hundreds of combinations tirelessly in a way that would be quite impossible for a human – another potential route in was found.

If one could surmise where a message had been sent from – this was one of the tricks of the Y Service – it might be possible to guess at keywords of a military or technical nature that might be repeated in the encoded message.

Young recruit John Herivel took this thinking a stage further with an extraordinary moment of revelation. In the winter of 1940, billeted in a small house in Bletchley, he had finished his shift at the Park and was now back in his landlady's front parlour.

It was a dark, freezing evening; outside, the snow was falling and in the snug front room, as the glowing coals ticked in the grate, Herivel found himself starting to doze. He began to dream: and in that moment, he awoke, and leaped from his chair.

He had suddenly seen an image of an Enigma operator: a typical German soldier. Herivel imagined this soldier setting up the Enigma machine for use – and either from tiredness or stress, choosing as the machine's settings the letters already in the machine's windows from the day before. Herivel calculated how this mistake might be detected and how it could then be exploited by the codebreakers. This fantastic and pivotal insight was called 'the Herivel Tip' and it was to prove invaluable.

In addition to this, there were other similar and sly psychological breakthroughs, involving getting into the heads of the Enigma operators. It was realised that some Germans might start messages with 'Heil Hitler!'; or their preamble might be conversational. There might be mentions of the weather or indeed mentions of girlfriends and opening messages might be sent twice as a test.

Meanwhile, Bletchely's card file index was filling daily with crucial additions: esoteric terms for military hardware that may be used in messages. There were many lateral approaches into piercing everyday communications sent by belligerent or even bored young German men.

The recruits to Bletchley were urged to bear in mind this image of an average German signals operative; they were also encouraged to make a study of German slang, with particular reference to bad language. For, as Keith Batey recalled, these operators might make their opening messages jokingly full of swear words. 'An oik is always an oik,' he said.

In broader terms, the Bletchley codebreakers – with the help of the upper-class debutantes who had spent their formative years in 1930s German finishing schools, going to dances with officers – immersed themselves in conversational German: the means by which military men might greet one another.

They homed in on certain words and phrases that officers in the field would commonly use to one another. The codebreakers would get hold of the Enigma traffic of the day, concentrating on the first communications. Then they took these words and phrases and fed them to Turing's bombe machines.

These were termed 'cribs'; they were the means by which the machines, being given possible combinations of encoded letters in short phrases, might motor through 17,576 possibilities, sometimes for hours if on a repeated run. If the hunch was correct, and the machine hit the code, the mechanism of the drums would stop.

The settings of the bombe machine would then be fed to the British equivalent of the Enigma machine. It was called 'Type-X', and the encoded message streamed through it. What it would produce, if all had been successful, was a message in recognisable German.

The next stage in the process was to pass the message to the translators. Among these, there would be young linguists who would be specifically looking out for technical terms – aeroplane parts, references to missiles, incredibly specific words – which would then be stored in an ever-growing card file index.

These terms would then be used as an additional lever; in encoded messages from the Luftwaffe for instance, such technical terms might be fed speculatively to the bombe machines.

And so it was that Bletchley Park, which had begun as a kind of cottage industry, very soon became a codebreaking factory.

It took a while for the codebreakers to warm up into regular, successful decrypts – not really until the Battle of Britain in the summer of 1940 – but thereafter their successes were coming on a daily basis. What had seemed a miracle at first even more miraculously then came to seem routine.

There were – of course – horrible setbacks. The codebreakers in Hut 8, led by Alan Turing, were leading the fight against the Nazi naval Enigma codes. These were especially crucial: in the war at sea, German U-boats were prowling the waters around Britain, and targeting shipping filled with vital supplies. As well as the hideous loss of life when torpedoes hit hulls, stocks of food, fuel, ore and equipment were also destroyed. If the U-boats were successful too often, Britain could have been starved into submission.

The codebreakers in Hut 8 faced an additional hurdle: for the head of the German navy, Admiral Dönitz, had a niggling sixth sense – quite unlike Hitler, Göring, Himmler or the others – that the codes were being broken.

He was sufficiently uneasy about this to order a further ramping up of Enigma security. An additional rotor was fitted to some of the naval code machines. The result at Bletchley was a terrifying nine-month-long code blackout. The potential number of encoded combinations had jumped up by many millions again. The bombes were not enough.

In a breathtaking act of bravery, the situation was saved by three British sailors. One night in 1942, a German U-boat was sinking in the Mediterranean: Colin Grazier, Tony Fasson and Tommy Brown plunged into the waters and into the stricken craft itself in order to salvage its Enigma machine and the related codebooks with the instructions on each day's settings. Even as water was pouring into the U-boat, Fasson and Grazier were determined not to leave until the material had been passed up to Brown, and thence to a whaler. A lurching judder: and suddenly the U-boat was plunging like a stone deeper into the darkness of the depths. Brown survived but Grazier and Fasson lost their lives retrieving the coding books that was to help save innumerable lives to come.

In our age of instant digital solutions, it now seems extraordinary that something as benign-looking as the Enigma machine – one might even call it a design classic – was the source of so much sacrifice. Yet the battle to unlock it led indirectly to the world that we now see.

So the puzzles in this section – while requiring neither machinery, nor the need to work through 159 million million million combinations – are an attempt, inspired by Arthur Scherbius's original concept, to capture some of the daunting prospect of his machines: puzzles that require a cool head and a steady hand – or should that be vice versa?

# 1

## X MACHINE

In the crossword below, all the letters have been replaced by numbers. We have put the letter X in place, which is number 1, to start you off. You can keep a record of these numbers and letters by using the grids below the crossword. Using logical deduction and language skills can you complete the 15 x 15 frame? Every letter of the alphabet is used at least once.

| 10 | 15 | 14 | 10 | 22 | 19 |  | 21 | 9 | 15 | 26 | 17 | 5 | 9 | 4 |
|----|----|----|----|----|----|----|----|----|----|----|----|----|----|----|
| 3 |  |  | 3 |  | 17 |  | 22 |  |  | 12 |  | 15 |  | 17 |
| 17 | 4 | 4 | 14 | 10 | 12 | 4 | 24 |  | 14 | 6 | 7 | 14 | 4 | 16 |
| 5 |  |  | 10 |  | 23 |  | 24 |  |  | 15 |  | 21 |  | 3 |
|  |  | 18 | 14 | 13 | 12 |  | 14 | 15 | 16 | 9 | 4 | 17 | 19 | 24 |
| 18 |  |  | 7 |  |  |  | 4 |  | 9 |  |  | 19 |  |  |
| 12 | 21 | 6 | 9 | 19 | 19 | 8 |  | 19 | 22 | 6 | 18 | 12 | 10 | 24 |
| 12 |  |  | 24 |  | 25 |  |  |  | 16 |  | 12 |  |  | 17 |
| 15 | 14 | 19 | 12 | 6 | 22 | 11 |  | 19 | 12 | 9 | 20 | 12 | 12 | 11 |
|  |  | 17 |  |  | 9 |  | 19 |  |  |  | 12 |  |  | 8 |
| 2 | 9 | 7 | 19 | 12 | 24 | 24 | 14 |  | 6 | 14 | 7 | 11 |  |  |
| 14 |  | 12 |  | 1 X |  |  | 10 |  | 9 |  | 7 |  |  | 19 |
| 7 | 12 | 4 | 16 | 24 | 3 |  | 10 | 14 | 4 | 2 | 12 | 24 | 24 | 17 |
| 17 |  | 10 |  | 15 |  |  | 12 |  | 18 |  | 15 |  |  | 16 |
| 14 | 5 | 12 | 15 | 9 | 24 | 14 | 15 |  | 14 | 1 X | 8 | 16 | 12 | 4 |

| 1 X | 2 | 3 | 4 | 5 | 6 | 7 | 8 | 9 | 10 | 11 | 12 | 13 |
|----|----|----|----|----|----|----|----|----|----|----|----|----|
| 14 | 15 | 16 | 17 | 18 | 19 | 20 | 21 | 22 | 23 | 24 | 25 | 26 |

| A | B | C | D | E | F | G | H | I | J | K | L | M |
|----|----|----|----|----|----|----|----|----|----|----|----|----|
| N | O | P | Q | R | S | T | U | V | W | X | Y | Z |

## 2
### RATION BOOK

The first commodity to be rationed in September 1939 wasn't food at all, but another vital item. This is the item in a). Can you then work out the food items that were also rationed?

**a)**  i ~ # ¢ ∞ §

**b)**  Ω ≈ ç ∞ √

**c)**  Ω ∫ # # ~ ¢

**d)**  μ ∫ Δ ≈ ¢

**e)**  ç ¶ ~ ~ μ ~

**f)**  ~ Δ Δ μ

**g)**  ÷ ~ ≈ #

**h)**  ÷ ≈ ¢ Δ ≈ ¢ ... √ ~

## 3
### CAPITAL CODE

You need to think straight in this assignment, and work out the coded message.

4442   13   302   41132   32   012

# 4
## CONNECTIONS

Look at the two lists of words arranged in alphabetical order. Using a word from each list, make pairs by inserting another word between them which ends the first word and starts the next. When you have done this rearrange the connecting words to reveal the message. Here are the number of letters in the link words, in message order: 2 / 2 / 3 / 5 / 2 / 4 / 3 / 2 / 4

| | |
|---|---|
| CART | GONE |
| COLTS | IRON |
| ERR | KEEPER |
| GREEN | NIGHT |
| GRUB | PRINT |
| HAT | RAW |
| HITHER | SLING |
| LIFE | SWAIN |
| UNDER | WARD |

# 5
## SET SQUARE

Here's a line of a poem, a famous first line of a book and a line of a song to decipher. Word breaks and grammatical signs are in place.

**a)**  13  35  33  15, / 21  43  24  15  34  14  32  54 /
12  35  33  12  44, / 11  34  14 / 21  11  32  32 /
35  34 / 44  32  35  51  22  23

**b)**  32  11  44  45 / 34  24  22  23  45, / 24 /
14  43  15  11  33  45 / 24 / 53  15  34  45 / 45  35 /
33  11  34  14  15  43  32  15  54 / 11  22  11  24  34

**c)**  14  35  34'  45  /  41  51  45  /  54  35  51  43  /
14  11  51  22  23  45  15  43  /  35  34  /  45  23  15  /
44  45  11  22  15,  /  33  43  44  /
53  35  43  45  23  24  34  22  45  35  34

CLUES:

1. The numbers go higher than 26, so this is clearly more than a number substitution.

2. The letters X and Y are both replaced by the same number.

3. What's the title of this puzzle?

# 6

## CARD CONUNDRUM

Even a relaxing game of cards gave a chance to leave a coded message for the residents of Bletchley Park. Look at the playing cards below, which were left on a table after a game of canasta.

What is the food related message they reveal?

# 7

## CODE WHEEL

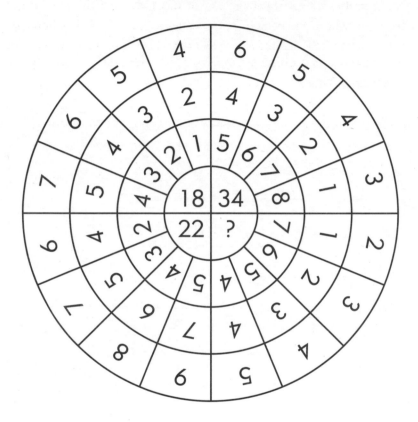

Which number is needed to complete the grid?

# 8

## DICING WITH DANGER

Any number of games make use of dice. Wartime games ranged from Pit, where you were a commodities trader, to Beetle where you tried to draw a six-legged insect on the roll of a dice. The inmates of Bletchley were playing far more dangerous games on a daily basis, as by solving the codes many lives were saved. The faces of the dice below reveal a simple but effective number code. Can you decipher the code and work out which numbers are in row 4? From there can you connect how this number was relevant to the second and penultimate years of World War II but not the remainder?

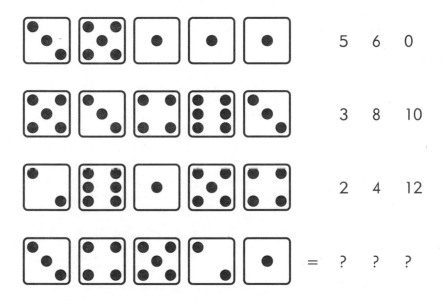

5 6 0

3 8 10

2 4 12

= ? ? ?

# 9
## THE UNKNOWN QUANTITY

This code is a straightforward substitution of numbers for letters. The code is the same in all the words. Which number should take the place of the question mark?

| | | | | | | | |
|---|---|---|---|---|---|---|---|
| **a)** | 1 | 4 | 4 | | | | |
| **b)** | 4 | 1 | 2 | 3 | 1 | | |
| **c)** | 3 | 5 | 6 | 4 | 3 | 2 | 1 |
| **d)** | 1 | 2 | 4 | 3 | 2 | 1 | |
| **e)** | 5 | 1 | 6 | 2 | 3 | 2 | 4 |
| **f)** | 3 | 2 | 6 | 2 | 1 | | |
| **g)** | 5 | 6 | 2 | 4 | 1 | | |
| **h)** | 1 | 2 | 3 | 4 | 5 | ? | |

# 10

## JIGSAW CODE

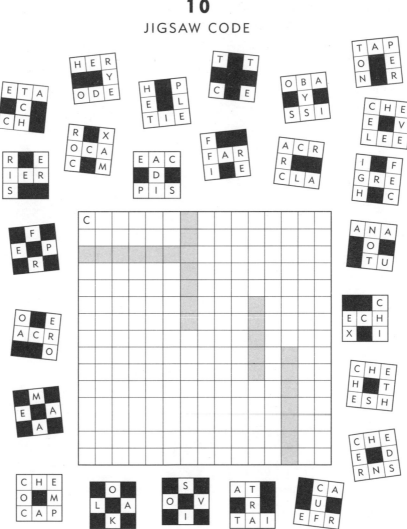

A completed 15 x 15 block of letters has been broken up into 25 squares. It is up to you to replace the squares in the correct positions to form words that interlink and read either across or down. As with a crossword, the pattern of words is symmetrical. In the completed grid, the letters in the shaded squares reveal an important coded message. The order of the words you need are to be read left to right, top to bottom. A letter C is in the top left-hand corner.

# CHAPTER FOUR

# MIND YOUR SECRET LANGUAGE

Even the whirlpool of chaos generated by the Enigma machine counts as the echo of language: an impossibly distorted echo, but still there in its essence – letters inscribed on paper.

The letters stand for other letters, and the words and sentences are broken down into clumps of five-letter groups. And you know that when you are looking at messages encrypted by Enigma, those letters chosen to represent the others are not perfectly random. There is a machine setting that will restore their meaning.

Even without that machine, you know that the words and sentences are still in there: the sequences are complete gobbledegook but the meaning is still hidden on that piece of paper.

This is why codebreaking was never solely a proposition for mathematics geniuses. The discipline also needed people who had a profounder feel than most for the internal rhythms and structures of language: not just English, or any of the other common tongues, but all languages. This is also why Bletchley's recruiters searched a little further afield than students of advanced algebra and geometry. They also hunted out the poets.

The puzzles in this section will test not specific language knowledge – that would be unfair – but instead will pose a deeper challenge to do with one's general feel for any language: even a nonsense one. Indeed, the invented language was one method later devised for the codebreaking directorate to pull in fresh recruits.

It was slightly more straightforward at the start of the war. One of Bletchley Park's great finds in 1940 was a young woman called Mavis

Lever. She had been studying at the University of London until war came, then her department was evacuated to the University College of Wales in Aberystwyth.

This was, and is, a particularly beautiful and wild spot, especially for the study of wild, soaring romantic German poetry – for German was one of Mavis Lever's specialities. Away from the soot and fog of London, Mavis was free to walk in the hills that surrounded the coastal town, or to roam for miles on the eerie empty sand dunes of Borth. But she felt there to be something utterly wrong about doing so. For, as she said, there was something awful about studying the most lyrical of the German poets while German pilots were preparing to unleash fiery hell across the cities of Britain.

So she swiftly decided to leave her studies behind and volunteer for war work. First of all, she had been set on training as a nurse but an old friend said, 'Oh no you don't,' and pointed her in the direction of occupations that could best use her powerful intellect. Mavis Lever's first war job was in Whitehall at the Ministry for Economic Warfare. Her analytic mind was noted, and one of her superiors, who happened to be an old friend of Dilly Knox, wondered whether she might be better serving the nation in an even more challenging role.

It was not long before Mavis Lever got the summons to report to 'Station X'. She arrived late one night, was escorted from the railway station to the big house nearby, and was asked instantly to sign the Official Secrets Act. Some in a similar position felt a little ambiguous about being thrown into this new life. But Mavis Lever was intensely glad.

What she and many other linguists brought to Bletchley Park was a flair as indispensable as that contributed by the mathematicians: because as well as every problem having a mathematical solution, Enigma codes always at their heart were language puzzles.

It is for this reason that so many of those who worked at Bletchley loved cryptograms and other word games. They would have loved Scrabble too – except by that stage it had not quite yet been invented. Early versions of the board game were around in America but it only emerged in its modern form after the war.

Nonetheless, what the linguists of Bletchley Park were doing was something not dissimilar: working with scrabbled individual letters.

Mavis Lever was sent to work in the Bletchley department known as 'the Cottage', a red-brick outbuilding just across the courtyard from the main house. This was the operational headquarters of the fearsomely eccentric Dilly Knox, for whom Mavis would find herself working.

Although the work and the discipline was a long way from the mist-enshrouded hills of Wales, Dilly Knox found a way to make the intellectual challenge of Enigma exciting in quite a different way.

Knox had developed a new system of encoded letter rearranging which he called 'rodding'. In essence, this was a slide rule that corresponded with encoded letters laid out in an alphabet square. No explanation can convey the initial complexity of the thing ('rodding' also involved 'comic strips' – that is, moveable strips of letters). But the idea fundamentally was that one did not need a machine the size of a wardrobe to unlock codes. Indeed, one could do it at one's dining table, if you were patient enough to write out strips of letters.

Such a technique also conveyed to Mavis Lever that codebreakers did not have to be acquainted with esoteric maths knowledge, such as Bayesian probability theory: that anyone with a love for language and letters could extend that fascination to the encrypted kind.

Mavis Lever swiftly demonstrated her aptness for the work. She set to work on burrowing into the Italian Enigma codes. In September 1940, working deep into the late summer night, she was examining an intercepted message which from earlier attempts to crack it appeared to start with the letters PERX.

This was no known Italian technical term; nor did it seem to be any form of acronym. But using a little guesswork, Mavis Lever wondered if – since this was the start of the message – there had been a little misunderstanding. And whether minus the erroneous X, those first several letters would lengthen out to become the word 'personale' – meaning 'personal' – as a means of kicking off the communication.

She was quite right; it was a personal message. (On another later occasion, she burrowed into a German coded message with the knowledge that the man who sent it had a girlfriend called Rosa, to whom he referred often.) And in order to test the Italian message theory out, she worked throughout the night unlocking letter after letter. Like the Germans, the Italians changed their Enigma settings every twenty-four hours, but with this discovery, Mavis Lever, applying Knox's methods, had established a principle that there were linguistic as well as algebraic means of prying open messages.

Some months later, after working on ever more codes, her ultimate triumph came: having deduced that an Italian naval message emanating from the Mediterranean read 'X minus three days', Mavis Lever correctly divined that something big was afoot. The Admiralty was alerted. That 'something big' was to blow up into the Battle of Cape Matapan and thanks to Mavis Lever's timely warning, the Royal Navy won the battle. She was thanked personally by Admiral Cunningham. She was still only twenty years old.

A little later, a young mathematician who was working in Hut 6 with Gordon Welchman caught Mavis's eye. Keith Batey, who had been lured to Bletchley from Oxford, was instantly taken with this brilliantly self-assured young lady. Romance blossomed, though the pair of them were forbidden from ever discussing what happened in their respective codebreaking departments. That was how tight security was: you could not even confide in colleagues or indeed in romantic partners.

Yet despite all the security concerns, the authorities generally were keen to encourage relationships; the work after all was so intense and the codebreakers needed to feel human. Mavis Lever and Keith Batey at first assumed that their relationship was itself top secret, but when they found places specially prepared for them side by side in the Bletchley Park canteen, they knew that nothing got past the Park's directorate.

In wider terms, Bletchley Park was lucky in its linguists: from novelist-to-be Angus Wilson (who found the work so stressful that he once threw an ink bottle at a Wren) to the poet F. T. Prince.

There were also some impressive intellects attached to Bletchley's sister department, the Radio Security Service, which was aiming to monitor communications from the Abwehr, the German secret service. Notable among them was a young don from Cambridge with a vitriolic sense of humour. Hugh Trevor-Roper (later Lord Dacre) was based in a special office in the evacuated west London prison of Wormwood Scrubs. He found himself facing all sorts of German hand-ciphers (those not generated by Enigma).

Trevor-Roper was a polymath: a historian of academic leaning, but also a mathematician of sorts. On top of this, he had a very fine working knowledge of the German language. Even though he wasn't supposed to, Trevor-Roper would take German ciphers back to his digs in the west London suburb of Ealing: as he listened to bombers flying overhead, he would concentrate hard on cracking the codes. His biographer Adam Sisman noted that these German ciphers provided a welcome alternative to *The Times* crossword: puzzle addiction taken to its ultimate extreme.

There were other figures too who had been codebreakers rather longer, and who were soon to help shape the future of Britain's secret relations with America. One such was a formidable eccentric called Hugh Foss: six foot five inches tall, reddish of hair, chaotic in domestic terms, but blessed with a pulsating intellect combined with raw curiosity.

Foss had been born in Kobe, Japan, to missionary parents; this was his first head start. He was at ease with Japanese at a time when there was barely a handful of people in Britain who could make such a claim. By the end of 1941, as the Japanese attack on the US naval base Pearl Harbor brought America into the war, this rare skill became vital to the codebreakers. The complexities of Enigma were one thing: the challenge posed by codes in Japanese were quite another.

Hugh Foss, who rose to become Bletchley's head of Japanese Section, was a man of unusual passions. He was obsessed with Highland dancing and was frequently to be seen wearing a kilt – despite the fact he was not actually, strictly speaking, Scottish. As we shall see in more detail later, before the war, Foss had brought the craze for Scottish reels to the smarter streets of Chelsea, forming a club for the pursuit and persuading fellow senior codebreaker Alastair Denniston and his wife to take part.

Foss also founded a magazine called *The Reel*. In this he wrote articles, devised new Highland reels (with dance-move diagrams that looked like codes), and also set logic and cryptogram puzzles.

For Foss, symbols created action: just as Highland dance diagrams translated into group spectacles of breathtaking elegance and speed, so the codes employed by the Japanese military mapped directly onto a world of kinetic violence.

His deepening knowledge of the Japanese language was a means of approaching military conundrums from another angle: to be fluent in a language is to see deeply into the heart of a culture, and the thinking that informs it. Different cultures have different approaches to such notions as the enemy, or even reasonable force. The way language is deployed can heighten aggression. For Hugh Foss to penetrate Japanese codes, he wanted to penetrate the Japanese military mind.

Elsewhere at Bletchley Park, senior codebreaker Colonel (later Brigadier) John Tiltman had impressively taught himself Japanese. He then set about ensuring that new recruits were taught the fundamental basics themselves; one Commander Tuck was put in charge.

Everything to do with Bletchley was top secret at all times, naturally: so the townsfolk of nearby Bedford could only speculate about the commander who had taken over rooms above the local gas showroom in the high street, and about the young men, some in uniform, some not, who were trooping in and out. This was the codebreakers' school of Japanese, and those recruited specifically for this area, such as Oxford undergraduate linguist Michael Cohen, found that it was the gateway into a new realm.

Not that the eleven-week course was in any way easy. Part of the tuition involved listening to gramophone records of simple Japanese conversation, running slowly and then at ever greater speed, and at some volume. It was said that either the intensive method worked brilliantly, or the students were carried out screaming.

Codebreaker Alan Stripp, another undergraduate, found that the confidence that came with mastering codes and languages of the Far East could then be applied elsewhere: he became an expert in Farsi, the language of Iran, and later in the war, he sailed to the Indian Ocean and travelled deep into the foothills of the northwest frontier to a secret listening station. From there he intercepted messages from Iran, Azerbaijan and Soviet forces in central Asia.

Meanwhile, among the Americans who were eagerly co-opted into Bletchley Park later in the war – working with some wonder in a realm of tweed and tea-breaks – was a brilliant young man called Arthur Levenson.

Levenson was a polymath, deeply versed in both mathematics and literature. During his time at Bletchley, he had a particular fascination for the works of the novelist James Joyce.

Joyce's earlier masterpiece *Ulysses* – 700 pages set in the course of a single day in Dublin, 1904 – is a book filled with mischievous, quite deliberate codes, notable among which is the recurring enigma of the postcard with the legend 'U.P: up', which has been sent to one of the characters. Entire academic papers have been devoted to the mystery of what it might mean.

Joyce's later masterwork, *Finnegans Wake*, is where he sets sail out on to the wider ocean of language: at first glance, all 500 or so pages of the book are impenetrable. Familiar words are conjoined to form new words; sentences drift and trail, changing sense as they go; there are anagrams and riddles and profoundly obscure references, both classical and mythological. Yet in all that rich and colourful chaos there is the maddening sense that a meaning can be divined and unlocked.

Arthur Levenson adored *Finnegans Wake* and you can see now why a codebreaker might relish the chance to square up to Joyce: the novelist's linguistic inventiveness and exuberance makes the challenge of unravelling his words so much more rewarding than any common cryptic crossword. For all his daunting reputation, Joyce was also terrifically witty.

A little after the war, when Bletchley Park had regenerated into the new department of GCHQ, the vital importance of linguistic skill was still recognised by senior codebreakers who had learned their trade in the grounds of the Park.

One new recruit in those post-war years recalled that he was set a most striking aptitude test to see if he would be suitable for cryptographic work.

He was sat down with a piece of paper, upon which appeared to be written pure gibberish. There were fragments of recognisable words, but mixed in with a swirl of what looked like random chaos, with a very faint scent of Old English about it.

There was an introductory note. The candidate was informed, in all seriousness, that he was looking at the language of the elves. This was the language that could, if one listened very hard, be heard deep in the forest. It was the candidate's task to translate what all the elves were saying.

Possibly there was a note of Tolkien in there (a favourite of code-breaking types); importantly, there was also a suggestion of James Joyce, and the multiple languages and references of *Finnegans Wake*.

The candidate settled down to this unusual and taxing exam. He was told shortly afterwards that he had passed successfully.

The candidate's name was David Omand. In time he rose to be head of GCHQ. The moral of the story is once again to do with the wide range of intellectual skills the codebreakers were looking for, together with the ability to tackle a seemingly impossible proposition not only with enthusiasm but also with a certain amount of humour.

So the puzzles in this section don't just have a strongly linguistic flavour: they also revolve around a completely made-up language! You are invited to familiarise yourself with the intriguing vocabulary of Kat and to translate the sentences into English (and English into Kat!). On top of that, in honour of the great James Joyce, there is also a short passage from *Finnegans Wake*, of the type so relished by Arthur Levenson.

# 1

## THE LANGUAGE OF KAT

All of the questions below are based on an invented language called Kat. Word order is different from that of English and there is no wrong or right order, so there are multiple solutions (for example, 'the mice are watching the cat' or 'the cat is watching the mice'). Start by reading the sample sentences in Kat for each section and then answer the following questions.

### SAMPLE SENTENCES 1

piacak kitegg tolg – The dog likes cats
kit grih mangak – The cat eats the mouse
persek tolg grih – The dog chases the mouse
woleeg uchakel toleeg – The ladies are walking the dogs
fel kitegg grihegg – The mice watch the cats
casal uchakel toleeg – The dogs are walking home
wolg kitegg persekel – The cats are chasing the lady
und toleeg kitegg wolg piacak – The lady likes the cats and dogs

**1**  Give the meaning of:

**a)**  casal toleeg und uchak kitegg

**b)**  griheeg felkel woleeg

**2**  Translate the following sentences into Kat:

**a)**  The cats and dogs like the lady.

**b)**  The dogs are chasing the cats home.

SAMPLE SENTENCES 2

kit toleeg persek ke – Two dogs chase the cat
uchak wolg mu toleeg – The lady walks three dogs
und wolg jonelegg kit fel – The lady and the children watch the cat
jonelegg fel wolg uchak casal – The lady watches the children walk home
kitegg grih fel fee – The mouse watches the four cats

**3**  Give the meaning of:

**a)**  mu casal woleeg ke persek toleeg

**b)**  grih kitegg fel ke

**4**  Translate the following sentences into Kat:

**a)**  The dog watches the cat and the cat watches the mouse.

**b)**  The dog and the cat watch the children walk home.

SAMPLE SENTENCES 3

pun kit mangak – The cat eats meat
persek tolg fu jonelegg kit da – The children chase the dog away from the cat
grih vinkel jonelegg – The children are stealing the mouse
grih uchak ro kit – The mouse walks on the cat
tolg vink pun da wolg – The dog steals meat from the lady
wolg casal piacakel ucha – The lady is liking the walk home

**5**  Give the meaning of:

**a)**  jonelegg und mu woleeg pun mangak

**b)**  casal tolg mangak ucha ro pun

**6**  Translate the following sentences into Kat:

**a)**  The lady watches the dog steal meat.

**b)**  The two cats chase the mouse away from the house.

# 2

## FINNEGANS WAKE

It is not documented how far the gifted American cryptographer Arthur Levenson managed to get in decrypting James Joyce's famously obscure masterpiece, published in 1939. But since then, countless readers, critics and indeed amateur cryptographers have been diving into *Finnegans Wake*, finding multiple interpretations of practically every word and phrase in the novel.

Here is the first page of the book. Your challenge: not only to fathom meaning, but also to catch the multiple geographical and literary references.

A few hints: these are (it is widely understood) the tumbling, dreaming thoughts of a sleeping man; and there are nods here to *The Book of Genesis*, Mark Twain, and the topography of Dublin.

riverrun, past Eve and Adam's, from swerve of shore to bend of bay, brings us by a commodious vicus of recirculation back to Howth Castle and Environs.

Sir Tristram, violer d'amores, fr'over the short sea, had passencore rearived from North Armorica on this side the scraggy isthmus of Europe Minor to wielderfight his penisolate war: nor had topsawyer's rocks by the stream Oconee exaggerated themselse to Laurens County's gorgios while they went doublin their mumper all the time: nor avoice from afire bellowsed mishe mishe to tauftauf thuartpeatrick: not yet, though venissoon after, had a kidscad buttended a bland old isaac: not yet, though all's fair in vanessy, were sosie sesthers wroth with twone nathandjoe. Rot a peck of pa's malt had Jhem or Shen brewed by arclight and rory end to the regginbrow was to be seen ringsome on the aquaface.

The fall(bababadalgharaghtakamminarronnkonnbronntonnerronntuonnthunntro varrhounawnskawntoohoohoordenenthernuk!) of a once wallstrait oldparr is retaled early in bed and later on life down through all Christian minstrelsy. The great fall of the offwall entailed at such short notice the pftjschute of Finnegan, erse solid man, that the humptyhillhead of humself prumptly sends an unquiring one well to the west in quest of his tumptytumtoes: and their upturnpikepointandplace is at the knock out in the park where oranges have been laid to rust upon the green since devlinsfirst loved livvy.

# CHAPTER FIVE

# THE CHESSBOARD WAR

Here are the words of a man who – arguably – steered Britain safely through the worst of the Battle of the Atlantic: 'My experience', wrote Conel Hugh O'Donel Alexander, 'is that it is very difficult to lose at chess with good grace.

'This is because chess being entirely a game of skill,' he continued, 'you cannot soothe your wounded vanity by thinking that the cards were against you, that you find grass so slow after hard courts, that the sun was in your eyes when you missed the catch – there are no extraneous influences on which your defeat can be blamed; you are the sole cause of your own downfall.'

He wrote this in one of his several books devoted to the art of chess. And of course, for chess, read codebreaking, for what Hugh Alexander carefully didn't mention in any of his books on how to play the game was that he was one of Bletchley Park's brightest stars.

He was also careful not to mention the fact that several other brilliant tournament chess players in Britain at that time had also worked at Bletchley Park. The game was practically the spine of the institution. To reflect this, the puzzles in this section will have a chess theme, including problems set by Alexander himself and a handy primer for those who are not hugely familiar with the game.

Strikingly, the talent-spotters for the wartime codebreaking centre knew very early on that they had to scout out the world of chess.

As George Atkinson wrote in his book *Chess and Machine Intuition*: '(Director Alastair) Denniston understood that chess players tend to make good cryptographers . . . both activities depend on trained intuition, the ability to recognise patterns within specific contexts.'

It was perhaps little wonder that the Bletchley department called the 'Government Code and Cypher School' – forming the acronym GC&CS – was affectionately nicknamed the 'Golf, Cheese and Chess Society'.

Of those chess masterminds scooped up for the Second World War, Hugh Alexander had been a junior champion in his youth, as had Stuart Milner-Barry and Harry Golombek. And of course the entire reason for their suitability can be found in that paragraph of Alexander's above: when faced with Enigma and other German encoded variations, the cryptanalysts had to bring not merely intellect alone, but also aggression, guile, a certain devilish glee and a fierce competitiveness.

Stuart Milner-Barry had, like Hugh Alexander, been a 'Boy Champion' at chess in the 1920s and the two got to know each other in university. Indeed, when war broke out on 3 September 1939, the pair of them were actually at an international chess tournament in Argentina; they immediately abandoned it to sail back to Britain on an eerily deserted cruise ship. Very shortly afterwards, they answered the call from Bletchley.

Milner-Barry later confessed that, although one should never really say this about war, he and Alexander had an exhilarating and comfortable time. The codebreaking problems really were like chess. Milner-Barry said: 'Both for Hugh and myself it was rather like playing a tournament game for five and a half years.'

As Hugh Alexander succeeded Alan Turing to become head of Hut 8 – dealing with naval Enigma codes – Milner-Barry was head of Hut 6, dealing with army and air force ciphers. They had both previously learned a valuable principle in their world of competitive chess: how to make light of the most intense pressure, while simultaneously using that pressure as a means of kick-starting the mind.

The ability to visualise as-yet-unmade chess moves; the ability to foresee the likely moves that your opponent might make; the ability to spot a potential solution to a seemingly insoluble problem – these were all weapons in the chess player's armoury.

Strikingly, given that he was by some distance Bletchley's most original thinker, Alan Turing was not especially good at chess. His colleague Peter Twinn recalled how sometimes, after shifts, they would go back to Twinn's digs in town and play. Twinn – who was only the most casual player of the game himself – frequently won.

Nonetheless, the game did have a powerful hold on Turing's imagination in another sense: shortly after the war, as he was working to bring his dream of a thinking machine into reality, Turing devised a then extraordinary computer program that would enable such a machine to play chess. The project was called Turo-Champ. These days the idea seems commonplace: before 1950, it was science fictional.

Turing also had competition from some other former codebreaking colleagues, who after the war had returned to academic careers in Oxford. Shaun Wylie – who was to be yanked back into the secret world by being offered the position of head of mathematics at the new GCHQ in the 1950s – was working on his own computer chess program together with another Bletchley veteran Donald Michie.

Their chess-playing computer project was called Machiavelli. And primitive though their machinery was – computers then were the size of cupboards, and could fill entire rooms, the labyrinths of their wiring trailing everywhere – the intellectual ambition was dazzling. Even to have come up with a machine that could 'think' one move ahead was an extraordinary achievement.

Wylie and Turing were rather tickled by the possibilities of their programs and had the idea that their rival computers could face each other in a chess challenge. How would machine play machine? Would that produce any evidence that these masses of circuits could in any possible sense 'think' a problem through?

Through correspondence, the two men set up the game and indeed their machines did come up with moves. The only difficulty was the time spent setting them up in order to do so; in an age when electronic miracles are performed on our phones in the blink of an eye, it is difficult to conceive of a time when computers were hot, noisy contraptions that smelled of oil and heated thermionic valves and when programming was a serious time-consuming endeavour. One chess move could take weeks, even months. After cajoling a few moves out of Turo-Champ, it was Turing who gave up the battle first, discouraged by the length of time it took.

Machines aside, Turing also happened to enjoy the game as a means of relaxation, while others seemed to enjoy taking him on for the challenge of pitting their intellects against his exceptional genius. At Bletchley, Turing was challenged to a match by one of the Park's most formidable champions. South London-born Harry Golombek had, before the war, become established as one of the world's brightest talents in the game, so his recruitment into the world of ciphers was a natural move. Golombek went a little easy on Turing during their matches across the board, but even so, Turing was never up to it.

A beguiling thing about these chess-players was that they came from a variety of backgrounds. Golombek's parents were Russian Jewish, having established themselves as grocers in south London at the turn of the century. Milner-Barry and Alexander came from middle-class, middle-England backgrounds. Yet before, during and many years after the war, they all remained extremely close-knit.

While the codebreaking that went on at Bletchley Park obviously remained a deep secret, it happened to be a secret that was known by Ian Fleming. The creator of James Bond, who had worked in naval intelligence throughout the war, was one of the tiny handful of people outside of Bletchley Park who was allowed in on the codebreaking efforts. Fleming was fascinated by the link between chess and codes, and in 1953, he was beguiled by the sensation caused at the Hastings International Tournament.

That year was the first that the Soviet grandmasters David Bronstein and Alexander Tolush came to Britain to play. And they found themselves up against the amused – and amusing – figure of Hugh Alexander.

The newspapers – with absolutely no idea of Alexander's top-secret shadow career breaking into Russian codes – reported on his matches with these chess titans breathlessly. And when he beat them both, Hugh Alexander became something of a modest national sensation.

It seems quite clear that Fleming lodged the match away in his creative imagination, for in his 1957 Bond novel *From Russia With Love*, there is a scene involving a Soviet chess champion cryptologist struggling to focus on a tense tournament match while being summonsed by the KGB villain Rosa Klebb. The real-life struggle between Alexander and the Soviets – a Cold War battle being fought across a chessboard – had clearly been the inspiration.

The apparent insouciance of Hugh Alexander – a trait he shared with other chess-players – was in its own way a means of holding on to sanity during wartime. Life in Hut 8 might otherwise have simply been too much: when German U-boats were sending precious lives and cargos to the bottom of the sea, Alexander and his team were under constant pressure from Downing Street to crack those U-boat codes and get fixes on their positions and courses.

The ability to play chess also relied on the ability to flick a mental switch. The problem in hand would receive full focus, but when off-shift, it was important to be able to shut it out. All-important was the capacity to relax and laugh. Hugh Alexander and Stuart Milner-Barry had a bit of a head start with this as they were billeted in one of Bletchley's most agreeable old pubs: the Shoulder of Mutton. Here they could relish the good local beer and the landlady's apparently very fine cooking.

In the later years of the war, another chess enthusiast, Donald Michie (who had been born in Rangoon and who came to the Park after showing a dazzling capacity for learning Japanese at speed), was working on the Colossus. This was the code-crunching machine that in essence kick-started the computer revolution. Chess was more than just a game to him: like his colleagues, Michie spent a huge amount of time brooding about the possibilities that a chess-playing computer might offer. It wasn't just about mechanical tactics or stratagems; it was about where such a leap might lead next. Some years after the war, Michie became renowned as a highly distinguished scientist: he and his wife were instrumental in pioneering the ideas and techniques of in vitro fertilisation.

An enthusiasm for chess was not confined to Bletchley's male codebreakers. Another addict was Hut 8's Joan Clarke, who would later become Alan Turing's fiancée for a short time. As well as being a genuine passion, a little friendly competition over the chessboard might also have been a means of Joan asserting her status as an intellectual equal among the men.

Chessboards were to be found in the main house, and in Hut 2, which had been set aside for recreation and beer-drinking. Indeed, it was through chess that Joan Clarke got to know Alan Turing better, their relationship in the truest sense a meeting of minds.

In the later years of the war, Bletchley Park's chess club was, ironically, the most distinguished in the country. Ironic, because none of the club's opponents were ever allowed to know exactly how these brilliant players were spending their war. In December 1944, the BP Chess Club was looking for fresh challenges and so took on the team at Oxford University. Naturally the Bletchley chess club triumphed. Given the top-secret status of the Park there must have been some bewilderment at this victory among the Oxford dons. In particular, as noted by author Christopher Grey, they must have wondered how it was that a small Buckinghamshire town known chiefly for its brick-making industry happened to be harbouring an extraordinary community of chess geniuses.

The puzzles that follow – while clearly not at the Grandmaster level, since that would hardly be fair – are ticklish enough to give an insight into tactics, strategy, and indeed the aggressive slyness of the codebreakers. Chess and cryptology alike were games that they could not bear to lose.

*If you have never played chess before, you can still tackle all the puzzles in this section. If you are more than a little rusty on the intricacies of the moves of individual pieces or you think the Sicilian Defence is an exotic cocktail, don't worry! All the information is provided in these pages for puzzle solving.*

# 1
## OPENING GAMBIT

Here's a chessboard set out for the opening of a game. Each player starts with eight pawns, one king, one queen, two rooks (or castles), two knights and two bishops.

Now here's a chessboard mid-game, where the remaining pieces are replaced by Xs. With the help of the clues, put all the pieces back in place and pinpoint the position of the two kings.

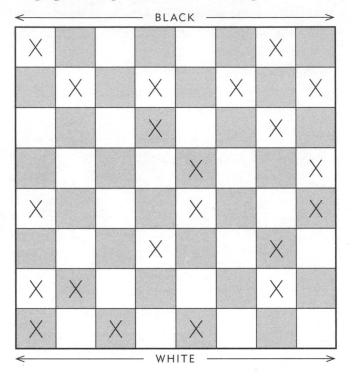

### CLUES

- White has lost three times as many pawns as black.

- Overall black has lost more pieces than white.

- Both black and white have five pieces that have not moved in the game.

- Both kings and queens are on the board, they have all moved and none are on a square matching their colour. In fact, all of the black pieces are on white squares.

- Looking across a row, or rank, of squares the two queens have each other in their sights.

- Pawns like to move forward (they're the only pieces that cannot move backward) and two pawns are the most advanced pieces down the board for black.

- The only knights remaining are two white knights, and one is the most advanced piece for white. Both knights are on black squares and they are the only coloured pair of starter pieces that remain on the board.

- Looking up and down the columns, or files, of squares there are seven times when two pieces with the same name appear in a file together.

# 2

## EXCHANGES

Change one word into another, moving a letter at a time. Below are clues to the words you need, but they are in no particular order AND there is a word included which won't fit in anywhere. What is it?

| *Exchange 1* | *Exchange 2* | *Exchange 3* |
|---|---|---|
| Manoeuvre WHITE TO BLACK: | Manoeuvre CHESS TO BOARD: | Manoeuvre MOVED TO PAWNS: |
| W H I T E | C H E S S | M O V E D |
| – – – – – | – – – – – | – – – – – |
| – – – – – | – – – – – | – – – – – |
| – – – – – | – – – – – | – – – – – |
| – – – – – | – – – – – | – – – – – |
| – – – – – | – – – – – | – – – – – |
| B L A C K | – – – – – | – – – – – |
| | B O A R D | P A W N S |

Here are the clues to the words you need plus one more:

| | | |
|---|---|---|
| Aperture | Pigs | Unruly children |
| Assignations | Make sense | Sunrises |
| Challenges | Crows | Insensitive |
| Mends | Young hen | Small pigeons |
| Metal | Travels | Chatter |
| Moan | Ships | Animal backbone |
| Salad ingredient | Adores | |

# 3

## MIDDLE GAME – KING'S GAMBIT

| K | N | I | G | H | T | | B | I | S | H | O | P | | Q | U | E | E | N |
|---|---|---|---|---|---|---|---|---|---|---|---|---|---|---|---|---|---|---|
|   |   |   |   |   |   |   |   |   |   |   |   |   |   |   |   |   |   |   |

The historic English village of Much-Cheating is home to a prestigious chess tournament. The event attracts interest from abroad, and it is suspected that one of the players may be using the meeting to pass on confidential information. The person playing white thinks he knows the name of the informer. He doesn't write down the actual name, but he has left a trail to find it from a sketch entitled KING'S GAMBIT.

What is the name of the informer?

# 4
## KNIGHT MOVES

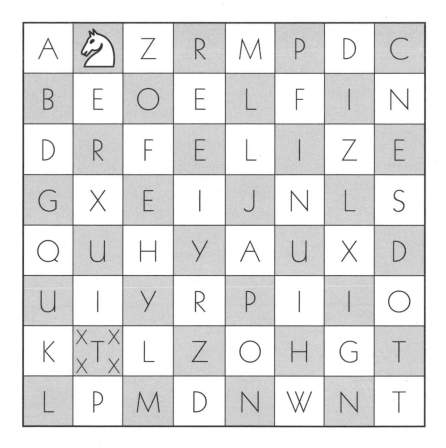

A knight moves three squares in the shape of an L, either one square up or down and two across, or two squares up or down and one across. Moving round this board can you collect the letters on the way and read the message issued by the British government in 1939? Each letter can only be used once but not all letters will be used. The final letter is marked by the Xs.

# 5
## ENDGAME

The words in the 'Endgame' column below are each the end of a chain of three words. Each word links to a word in the middle column, and although you can't see these words they will be in alphabetical order when you have worked them all out. You then have to find a chess-linked answer for the first column that links with the middle column. Fiendish!

| WORDS USED IN CHESS | LINK WORD | ENDGAME |
|---|---|---|
| | | CARD |
| | | ROADS |
| | | HALL |
| | | POST |
| | | WINK |
| | | CIRCLE |
| | | TICKET |
| | | DUTY |
| | | KEEPER |
| | | PLUM |

CHAPTER SIX

# THE CODES
# FROM THE
# MUMMY'S TOMB

Buried beneath the baking dust of Crete, and originally unearthed at the turn of the century by archeologist Arthur Evans, were thousands of clay tablets bearing a language unknown to any scholar. More discoveries, made later, revealed a similar though evolved language. These tablets were known as Linear A and Linear B. To decrypt these mysterious writings would be akin to the ability to climb into a time machine: to gain a glimpse of a long-vanished world.

More than anything, this was a codebreaking proposition. The tablets under the heading 'Linear B', a blend of pictograms and script assumed to be in Mycenean Greek, became an obsession for a young classicist called Michael Ventris. In the early 1950s, he became almost a household name as he cracked the ancient language, partly through intuiting place names. The doubly interesting and significant point is that he was enthusiastically helped by an academic called John Chadwick, a man who had honed and developed his codebreaking skills while working on Japanese ciphers at Bletchley Park.

The puzzles in this section have been formulated to reflect a largely unsung Bletchley recruitment trick: to seek out people who – like Indiana Jones – could examine ancient papyrii, or mysterious carvings on sacred stones, and summon forth their long-vanished meanings.

One particular route to a Bletchley Park posting was via the enigmas of Egypt: students and academics who were exceptionally adept at deciphering and reading ancient hieroglyphs on the walls of the tombs of the pharaohs – birds, cats, sidelong figures, hyena-headed deities – were considered suitably talented to attack German codes.

This was how it happened for a young man called Alec Dakin. 'In April 1940, about the end of the phoney war, Hugh Last, Camden Professor of Ancient History, asked me to come to his rooms in Brasenose College, Oxford,' Dakin wrote. 'He explained to me in a roundabout way that there was important but highly secret war work to be done, and that my studies in ancient languages and Egyptology might make me suitable for it.' That suitability saw him whisked along the then railway line that ran from Oxford direct to Bletchley.

Other Egyptologists pulled into code work included Paul Smither (sadly to die of leukaemia in 1943) and John Barns. These were men who were accustomed to dealing with ancient symbols and languages long extinct, which they sought to resurrect.

Before being co-opted to Bletchley they would have faced mysteries such as the meaning of the Rosetta Stone – a decree from the Ptolemaic dynasty carved into black granodiorite around 150BC in both ancient Egyptian and ancient Greek. This extraordinary artefact, discovered in 1799, was the gateway into deciphering that mysterious universe of hieroglyphs: the key to a lost language and by extension a lost world. Egyptologists were in a sense both codebreakers and time travellers. In this, they were continuing a fine codebreaking tradition: ancient texts in extinct tongues were after all the highly specialised area of Alfred Dillwyn ('Dilly') Knox.

When Knox was a young classicist at King's in 1909, he made it his business to decipher surviving papyrus fragments by the Greek poet Herodas. This required not merely deep linguistic knowledge but also – since he was working with ancient remnants – a flair for wildly imaginative guesswork too. If one could let one's mind roam with the possibilities of what filled those gaps in the papyrus text, one might unlock the entire document.

What possibly made this particular enigma a trifle easier on Knox was the colourful nature of the tales that Herodas was weaving. They involved everything from slavery to sex, brothels to flagellation. Knox spent many hours and weeks and months in the British Library reading room in Bloomsbury poring over this ancient puzzle. This work attuned him to the codebreaker's similar gift for wandering imaginative guesswork. Knox was first pulled from the British Library into the Admiralty in 1914; he was required in the cipher department ID25, known as Room 40. He was selected through academic and family connections; codebreaking was always a tight-knit circle.

It was in these dusty Whitehall corridors and rooms that Knox's manifold eccentricities began to set and harden. For instance, there was a bath at the end of a corridor (for its own obscure reasons) and Knox would brood on a cryptographical problem for hours in the water. Occasionally he would be found standing naked in the bath, as though he had forgotten to sit down.

Once more, the link with puzzles was strong: as the Great War went on, there were codebreakers established in all corners of the British Empire, and the one great connecting passion was a gift for riddles and cryptograms. In 1919, as many left the Whitehall department to return to civilian life, the cryptanalysts left behind a hand-made scrapbook (now sadly lost) which they had filled with puzzles in all sorts of languages – and ones that they had devised involving ancient Egyptian hieroglyphs.

Meanwhile, a centuries-old puzzle – in the form of a rather beautiful book – had surfaced in America. In 1912, an antiquarian book-dealer had happened across an extraordinary treasure. It was a richly colourful medieval book filled with illustrations of herbs, written in a coded language that no one could even begin to decipher. It took many years for word of this mysterious book to spread, but as it did, it came to obsess codebreakers on both sides of the Atlantic. And eventually, some thirty years later, efforts to decipher this exquisite mystery pulled in the senior Bletchley codebreaker Brigadier John Tiltman, as well as his opposite number in the American codebreaking department at Arlington Hall.

For while the Enigma codes were about the desperate need to destroy Nazism and influence the course of the future, the cipher contained in what became known as the Voynich manu-script offered the extraordinary possibility of completely rewriting western history.

The mystery began when, as Tiltman wrote, 'a vellum book of over 200 pages' was acquired in 1912 by Wilfred Voynich while he was in Italy. The cipher of the text proved beyond him. 'From 1912 to 1919,' wrote Tiltman, 'Voynich attempted to interest scholars in Europe and America in solving the script, while himself trying to determine the source of the manuscript.'

The book had popped up in historical accounts. There was a record of it dating back to 1666, when it was sent from Prague by university rector Joannes Marcus Marci to a fellow academic in Rome called Athanasius Kircher. Marci, it was noted, had been an expert in Egyptian hieroglyphics.

'This book, bequeathed to me by an intimate friend, I destined for you, my very dear Athanasius, as soon as it came into my possession,' wrote Marci in a covering letter, 'for I was convinced that it could be read by no one except yourself . . . the former owner of this book asked your opinion . . . To its deciphering he devoted unflagging toil . . . and he relinquished hope only with his life.'

But then the book – and the attempts to unlock its mysteries – were traced yet further back in time. In the sixteenth century, it had apparently belonged to Rudolph, King of Bohemia, who was tantalised by the alien language accompanying the exquisite coloured drawings of herbs and plants.

So who then was thought to be the author of this mysterious work of enigmatic beauty? One early theory was that it dated back to the thirteenth century, and was the work of the English scholar Roger Bacon. Yet the text apparently contained coded references to technological developments of which Bacon could have known nothing. Nothing, that is, unless such knowledge already existed in secret and hermetic form.

The bookseller Wildred Voynich was not shy about emphasising the mystery of his discovered manuscript: and he priced it very highly accordingly. 'When the time comes,' he told the press, 'I will prove to the world that the black magic of the Middle Ages consisted in discoveries far in advance of twentieth-century science.'

Such catnip set the experts salivating, especially the cryptographers. Among the first begging to be allowed to study the book was Professor William Newbold, who taught moral and intellectual philosophy at the University of Pennsylvania.

By 1921, he claimed that he had unlocked a part of the secret code. Then his claims went further: that indeed the book proved – unsettlingly – that Roger Bacon was writing about science quite unknown in the thirteenth century.

Professor Newbold made the announcement that the partial decipherments he had made pointed to an advanced working knowledge of astronomy, despite the fact that there were no telescopes in Bacon's day. He also claimed that one of the accompanying illustrations depicted the Andromeda spiral nebula.

'The world of American cryptology,' wrote Eamonn Duffy in a recent article on the Voynich manuscript, '. . . was saturated with conspiracy theories and fascination with the idea of hidden mysteries in ancient texts.'

By the late 1930s, the book had caught the attention of William F. Friedman, America's foremost cipher genius. When he was not leading team assaults upon Russian and Japanese coded messages, he was becoming increasingly beguiled by the manuscript: the mesmerising illustrations of everything from astrological wheels to embryos, and the text itself, which so maddeningly resembled recognisable language but then upon second glance proved itself utterly opaque.

The conspiracy theories had picked up some pace. Professor Newbold's claim of partial decipherment was proven false. As indeed was the dating of the book: it was established as a fifteenth-century production, coming nearly 200 years after Roger Bacon. But this simply stoked the fire of speculation. Could it possibly have been the case that Leonardo Da Vinci was the secret author of this work of art?

If there was an answer, it would only be found in the obscure language. As William Friedman became more and more absorbed by it, so his colleagues at the Arlington Hall codebreaking centre in Virginia were similarly pulled in. Surely the finest, sharpest codebreaking minds of the twentieth century could not be outwitted by a 600-year-old cipher?

It was in this spirit that Friedman turned to Bletchley's Brigadier Tiltman after the war. Even though Tiltman was fully engrossed in helping to regenerate Bletchley Park into a peacetime codebreaking department, he could not resist spending his off-duty hours pondering the Voynich challenge, and he was to ponder it for a good many years to come.

He had no time for the theories of Professor Newbold. But he was a little struck by the thesis of Dr Leonell Strong, who had been studying one particular page of the manuscript, dominated by a beautiful illustration of a sunflower. Dr Strong claimed that he had deciphered some passages, and that they had come out as medieval English. Tiltman said that he could not follow the logic of Dr Strong's deciphering methods and that 'his medieval English is not acceptable to scholars'. But Dr Strong was ascribing the book's authorship to a sixteenth-century 'physician and clergyman' called Anthony Askham, and this caught Tiltman's eye.

While diving deep into the coding possibilities, Tiltman ferreted about in academic libraries for any examples of the work of Askham. He came up with a book from the 1500s entitled *Banckes's Herbal*, which was attributed to Askham. The introductory text read: 'A little herbal, of the properties of herbs, newly amended and corrected, with certain additions at the end of the book, declaring what herbs hath influence of certain stars and constellations, whereby may be chosen the best and most lucky times and days of their ministration, according to the moon being in the signs of heaven . . .'

One thing that Brigadier Tiltman had been particularly noted for at Bletchley Park was his voracious appetite for learning, and his exploration of the Voynich manuscript led him off down similarly unexpected paths. He reported back to his friend Friedman that his textual analysis of the code had somehow made the maze even more complicated.

'My analysis, I believe,' Tiltman wrote a little later, 'shows that the text cannot be the result of substituting single symbols for letters in the natural order. Languages simply do not behave in this way.'

So what was this book really about then? Tiltman and Friedman discussed it further. Friedman had a theory that was a more concrete version of the Elizabethan mathematician, astronomer and occultist Dr John Dee's 'lost language of the angels'; he had been thinking of a man called Cave Beck, a seventeenth-century member of the Royal Society in London who had been obsessed with constructing a 'universal language', one that would cross all borders and cultures. Cave Beck had written in 1667: 'This last century of years, much has been the discourse and expectation of learned men, concerning the finding out of a universal character.'

Similarly obsessed with this universal language at roughly the same time was one Bishop Bedell, of whom it was written: '. . . the Bishop, finding the man had a very mercurial wit, and a great capacity . . . proposed to him the composing of a universal character, that might be equally well understood by all nations; and he showed him that since there was already an universal mathematical character, received for Arithmetick, Geometry and Astronomy, the other was not impossible to be done.'

Tiltman, meanwhile, was focusing his attentions on the herbs and astrology in the book, leading him into an exquisite world of ancient illuminated manuscripts: the medical use of plants as described in AD63 by the Greek gardener Krateuas, and the Roman *Anicia Juliana Codex*, written in about AD500. Yet even while exploring these and later medieval herbal books, Tiltman could not find any connection to the Voynich manuscript.

'To the best of my knowledge,' he wrote, 'no one has seen any book, certainly no illustrated book, of the period which covers the wide range suggested by the drawings in it.'

Added to this, he was forced to conclude that there 'is as yet no solid evidence that the manuscript is not by Roger Bacon or a copy of a work by him'. The Voynich manuscript was in fact carbon-dated some decades later: this proved it was produced in the fifteenth century, but as Tiltman said, that would not rule out the book being a facsimile of an earlier text.

And there is a further curious feature about this manuscript, which now sits in the library of Yale University: it has recently been pointed out that for a herbal directory, the book has one enormous flaw. None of the illustrations of herbs remotely resemble any real herbs. It is not just that the drawings might be seen as slapdash; it is that they are floridly imaginative. Fronds wave over impossible multiplicities of roots. And so if these are not real plants, then what is it fundamentally about?

The Voynich manuscript remains a mystery, continuing to tantalise scholars and theorists around the globe and inspiring several contemporary works of fiction. Tiltman and Friedman did not manage in the end to unlock its secrets, though their dogged persistence in pursuing all leads is typical of the mindset of the cryptanalysts.

The essential point here is to show the codebreakers' approach to historical challenges, and the terrific amount of scholarship that often went with it: whether poring over the intricacies of ancient Egyptian society, or studying the symbolism of the mandrake root in the medieval mind, the codebreakers of Bletchley Park epitomise the purest human curiosity.

And so the puzzles in this section are designed to replicate that innate pleasure in centuries-old mysteries: hieroglyphs, with clues and keys, that not only stimulate the eye and the imagination, but also hint at a new (while impossibly old) way of looking at language and communication. The symbols are real. In one of the cradles of civilisation, this was how thought was transmitted. The codebreakers understood that the ability to interpret unearthed texts was also to get close to a near-mystic ability to see through ancient eyes. They knew that language in any form actively shapes and changes the world whenever it is read.

# 1
## SIGN HERE

A certain number of symbols are painted on a tomb wall. They are made up of the same pictorial elements.

Which sign is missing?

# 2
## THE FIRST DIG

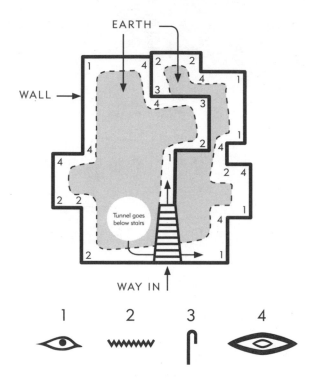

The tombs of ancient Egyptian Pharaohs house treasure beyond our imagination. But actually finding these sealed, secret rooms in a vast underground maze of tunnels was a challenge in itself.

Our sketch shows a plan of underground excavations. The digging has revealed a large complex with a stone wall leading from the entrance, as well as surrounding the edges. The Pharaoh who designed this vast burial vault for himself was known to be deeply interested in the powers of reason and logic. The numbers on the diagram indicate the hieroglyphs that appear on the tunnel walls. Surely, the diagram holds a key to locating where the hidden tomb is to be found?

# 3
## ON REFLECTION

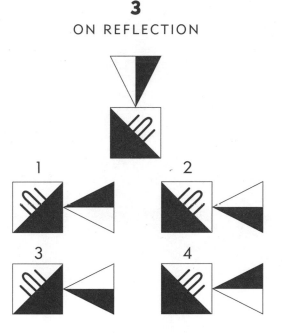

Metal mirrors were used in ancient Egypt. If the hieroglyph design shown at the top was turned 270 degrees clockwise and held in front of a mirror, which of the designs 1, 2, 3 or 4 would be reflected?

# 4
## RESEARCH NOTES

Research notes can be methodical and clear. At the same time they can be as obscure as the puzzle that is being solved. A distinguished linguistic expert who specialises in ancient languages has made the jottings below. What was she thinking about?

**a)** AM I MAD? I PRAY I MAY RIP MY DIARY!

**b)** FROM USED REFITTINGS, TREASURE RESTORES CINEMA

**c)** CAT WON DAN VOLES SEAMING!

# 5
## RESTORATION

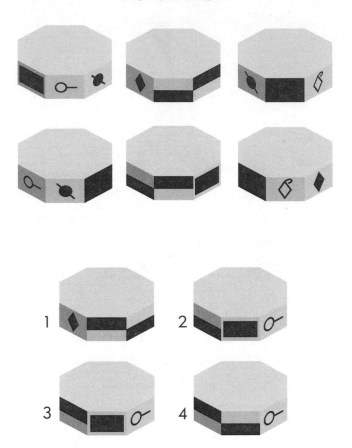

Here are some hieroglyphs viewed from different sides of the top of a column. Which of the patterns 1, 2, 3 and 4 corresponds to the markings on the column?

# 6
## PYRAMID BUILDING

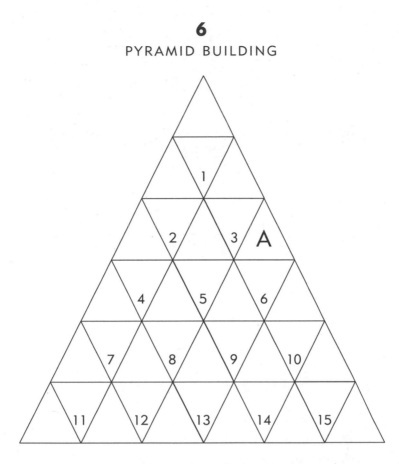

Fit all the listed words back into the pyramid frame. The first letter of each word is in one of the numbered triangles, the second is immediately above it, the third is immediately to its right and the fourth and final letter is to its left. There is a one-letter start. When all fifteen words are used and the grid is complete, a code word with an ancient Egyptian link can be discovered. And remember, there are often different ways of looking at things . . .

ANTI   ARIA   BEAT   CONE   DISC   GLEN   LIRA   ORAL
PACA   SLAB   SOLO   STAR   VEIL   WARE   ZERO

# 7
## EYE OF HORUS

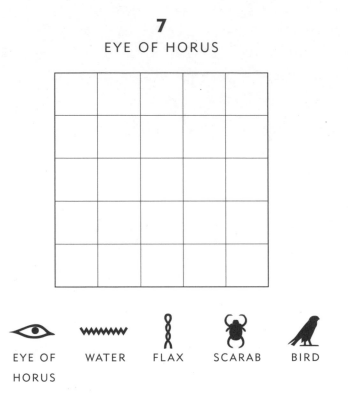

EYE OF      WATER      FLAX      SCARAB      BIRD
HORUS

A piece of papyrus is being pieced back together. There is a great debate about where certain hieroglyphs appear. The professors, academics and experts make the following comments.

Amazingly, for an intellectual debate, they are all correct in what they state.

Where will the eye of Horus appear?

**1.** There are five different hieroglyphs in this picture. The eye of Horus will feature once and once only. It is quite obvious to me that there must be at least one symbol between it and any bird image. All the birds must appear in the same column. They start below a scarab beetle.

**2.** The hieroglyph for water appears twice as often as the twisted flax. The water symbols are never in adjacent areas. One row features the flax symbol three times.

**3.** No two elements appear the same number of times and only one element appears in all the corners.

**4.** All of the scarab beetles will take up one whole row, plus one whole column.

**5.** Only one flax symbol appears in the pattern in any area that is on the right of a bird.

# 8
## HIDDEN MEANINGS

The whole study of fragments of information from long-gone civilisations involves the ability to seek things out that have been long hidden. Any other approach would leave answers to questions lost for ever in a burial vault! Can you find the secret words within these statements?

**a)** Examples of stucco designs have been excavated from ancient civilisations.

**b)** I saw Tom before anybody else saw him.

**c)** In many a malady nasty symptoms are prevalent.

**d)** Many have made a pilgrimage to Muscat, a combination of different periods of history.

**e)** Farmers who grow barley expect good crops and have done so for thousands of years.

**f)** Besides the carved name an ingot of pure gold had been placed.

# 9
## MUMMY'S MENU

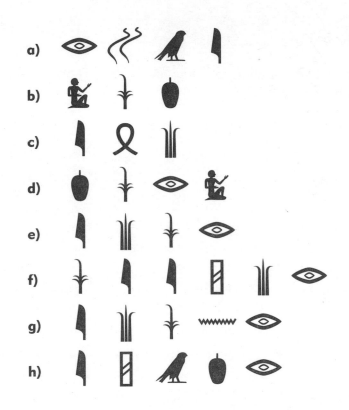

It's an early autumn day and the code crackers decide it would be fun to make some changes to the canteen menu. Using hieroglyphs to directly replace English letters, they produce the 'Mummy's Menu'. The names of the fare on offer may now look distinctly mysterious and exotic, but the food itself will be recognisable items!

# 10
## THREE-SIDED

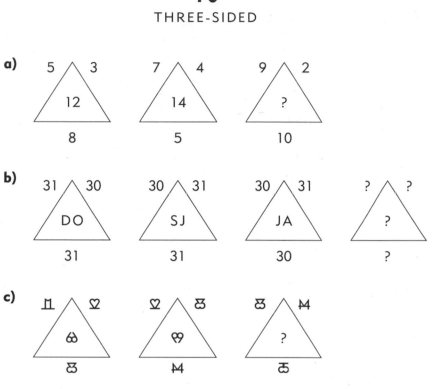

**a)**

5 △ 3
12
8

7 △ 4
14
5

9 △ 2
?
10

**b)**

31 △ 30
DO
31

30 △ 31
SJ
31

30 △ 31
JA
30

? △ ?
?
?

**c)**

♏ △ ♍
♋
♉

♍ △ ♒
♌
♈

♒ △ ♓
?
♊

Can you solve the pyramid patterns?

# CHAPTER SEVEN

# MUSIC, MAESTROS!

One of the curiosities of Bletchley Park was the very high proportion of codebreakers who were innately musical. This did not just mean that they could hold a tune. Many of them had an extraordinary ability to understand and feel the rhythms and structures of music. So the puzzles in this section will reflect not only that but also give a taste of the historical codes that some composers worked deliberately into their symphonies, leaving friends to decipher the messages amid the melodies.

The profusion of music in Bletchley Park was really quite exceptional. Senior cryptographer Gordon Welchman recalled coming off duty one summer's evening and taking a walk along the path of the Grand Union Canal. The rosy air of sunset was filled with the rather startling sound of a medieval choral harmony. He rounded a corner and in that rich warm light, he saw a party of codebreakers gathered by the water, singing madrigals.

The lives of Bletchley's young recruits were steeped in melodies old and new; many of the Wrens, billeted at Woburn Abbey, were passionate about the sound of Glenn Miller. Indeed, when he gave a concert at nearby Bedford, Wrens from codebreaking outstations dotted around the country were desperate to go and see him and his band.

There were more highbrow musical tastes at Bletchley too. In the middle of the war, the tenor Peter Pears (partner of Benjamin Britten) and the pianist Myra Hess were invited to perform at Bletchley Park. Neither artiste was given the slightest clue about what the Park was, or what sort of work their young audience was engaged in.

In addition to providing an appreciative audience, Bletchley had a rich array of musical talent all of its own: women and men who – after the war – would take prominent places in Britain's cultural landscape. There was James Robertson, who ran the Bletchley Park Choral Society; he had started his war in the Royal Air Force before being drafted over to the codebreaking side. The war had interrupted his orchestral career. Afterwards, he went to London to become musical director of the Sadler's Wells ballet company.

There was also a young composer who had been drafted into the RAF in 1943 as an eighteen-year-old and who was then transferred to Japanese codebreaking duties at Bletchley Park. This was James Bernard, who as a promising youngster had maintained a musical correspondence with Benjamin Britten. His work at Bletchley on the 'Purple' ciphers was very valuable but after the war he was at last free to join the Royal College of Music. Just a few years after that, he was composing – among many other brilliant film scores – the percussive pulsing music that accompanied the Hammer Horror films. He was responsible for cinema audiences peering through their fingers at *Dracula: Prince of Darkness*, *Frankenstein Must Be Destroyed* and *The Devil Rides Out*.

More film scores came from a popular Intelligence Corps operative called Herbert Murrill – before the war he had provided music for two cinema dramas. His real passion, though, was for grander orchestral and organ work, and it was to this that he returned after the war. Indeed, even during the conflict, he was given some responsibility for taking care of the BBC orchestra; handily, all its members had been evacuated to Bedfordshire, so he was close by to make sure that they kept up with rehearsals.

Even though music was so integral to Bletchley, it could still cause moments of surprise. On one occasion two young debutantes, new to the Park and adjusting to its eccentricities, walked past a khaki tent that had been set up relatively close to the huts. From within came the achingly beautiful sound of a piano being played. When they looked inside to find out what was going on they discovered a soldier called Wilfred Dunwell – recently drafted into codebreaking – at the keys. Dunwell was not just randomly talented; he also happened to be a professor at the Trinity College of Music, and later went on to write a book entitled *Music and the European Mind*. It was hardly what you would expect to stumble across in a military tent in Buckinghamshire.

There were intense musical gifts amongst the debutantes too. One of the Park's brightest sparks was a young lady from leafy Highgate in north London called Jane Fawcett. Before she had been recruited to the Park by Stuart Milner-Barry, she had started training as a ballerina. This, it seemed, was not destined for success – she was deemed too tall for this particular art form – but she could sing, and beautifully. So much so that when her time at Bletchley Park came to an end in 1945, she almost immediately enrolled at the Royal Academy of Music. This led to a successful career as an opera singer. She was noted for her interpretation of Scylla in *Scylla et Glaucus*. Another memorable performance came with a production of Henry Purcell's *Dido and Aeneas*.

So how might a feel for music dovetail into a genius for codes? Even as early as the 1920s, American cryptographers were exploring the way the mind worked, and how certain sorts of intellect responded to the strict structures of melodic composition. In Moscow, meanwhile, their Russian counterparts had also noticed this musical correlation.

In fact, long before Bletchley, composers were using their music as a means of transmitting specific messages as a sort of game. Edward Elgar loved cryptographic puzzles, and he was adept at smuggling words by means of musical notes into his work. The notes would come with a key, whereby 'A' would become 'E', for example. Then the notes would be played in specific sequences that would eventually spell a word out. By this means, Elgar was able, ironically enough, to spell out the word 'Enigma' in *The Enigma Variations*. In other works, he used musical notes to slyly spell out the names of friends, by means of a secret dedication.

Incidentally, Elgar also invented a code that no one to this day has been able to crack. It came in a letter that he sent to his friend Dorabella Penny in 1897. It consists, essentially, of elegant but baffling pen squiggles which may or may not be part of a letter substitution system. Certainly Dorabella Penny herself could never fathom its meaning. Nor for that matter can modern-day codebreakers.

Elgar was by no means alone in the game of burying codes within musical scores: the French composer Camille Saint-Saëns took a certain delight in it, as indeed did Johannes Bach. Meanwhile, in the world of popular culture, the idea of musical codes beguiled the film director Alfred Hitchcock. In his 1938 comedy thriller *The Lady Vanishes*, the titular vanishing lady has been attempting to get out of a central European country back to Britain with a vital secret message. All we in the audience know is that the night before, the lady had been listening to a folk singer beneath her hotel bedroom window. Then the folk singer was murdered.

Of course it transpires in the end (spoiler alert!) that the folk singer's melody was the message, one which, when played on a piano in the Foreign Office in London, can finally be decrypted. It was a neat plot device, though Hitchcock might not have known that such a novel encryption method had actually been around for centuries.

The chief difficulty with musical ciphers is that they can lead to an unearthly cacophony. It is one thing to transpose letters into musical notes; it is quite another to make those musical notes, when played in a sequence, artistically pleasing. The other option – embedding a message within an existing melody such as a folk song – is also rather limiting. If the notes cannot be varied, then neither can the message, meaning there are only so many words or sentiments one can hope to convey.

Nonetheless, given the clear symbiotic link between musical talent and codebreaking flair, it is not surprising so many efforts have been made to combine the two disciplines. That link is related to both linguistic and mathematical skill; the structures of music are deep and like any mathematical models, there are symmetries, resonances and surprising relationships. In addition, musical notation is itself a language; to anyone untrained, it might as well be the lost language of the elves.

As with music, and language, the ability to break into a cipher is related to a talent for feeling or seeing regularities and rhythms.

Perhaps it is more than that too: for to play music is to simultaneously focus and yet plunge into an abstracted world. There is perhaps an element of rapture there when clear meanings start to materialise from a cacophony of chaos.

At Bletchley, those musical talents needed to express themselves. Rather magnificently, in the later years of the war, they did so while simultaneously raising money for the war effort. As one codebreaker recalled, 'I played in the Chamber Music Group. Andre Mangeot came once a week to train us.' There was a general community hall built on the estate's Wilton Avenue and this was where the recitals would take place. 'Once the hall was built,' the codebreaker continued, 'we performed concert versions of *Figaro*, *Don Giovanni* and *The Bartered Bride* etc . . . also full versions of *Dido and Aeneas*. Frank Howes, *The Times'* music critic, came down to hear us and gave a glowing report.'

One pleasing element of this was that Howes would have had no idea what sort of work these young performers were doing when they were not playing. He might simply have assumed that – like the BBC orchestra – these were performers who had been evacuated.

Meanwhile, the pop singer Olivia Newton-John was taken aback to discover a few years ago that her father Brin had been a leading light at Bletchley Park, not merely for making serious inroads into Enigma traffic using his deep knowledge of German, but also because of his dazzling musical performances out of hours.

Brin Newton-John's mother – the family lived in Wales – was a member of the Royal Welsh Ladies Choir. Brin, when young, developed a keen aptitude for the violin. At the outbreak of war, he had gone into the RAF, and his experience of working with captured German pilots and a flair for intelligence led to him being seconded to Bletchley Park. Like everyone else, he needed some kind of a vent for the terrific pressure that he and his colleagues were under on a daily basis, and for Newton-John, this came in the form of singing in operas and giving memorable performances of German lieder (a principled choice, it might be said, during a time of war).

His name is now to be found in the archives on the programmes that accompanied Bletchley's concerts, recitals and revues: the townsfolk of Bletchley and members of the press who came to see the shows put on by these mysterious young people would have associated his name with a certain kind of highbrow entertainment, a long way from the popular culture fixtures of George Formby and Gracie Fields.

Structure – or the freeform lack of it – also played a part in the Park's musical life. Codebreaker Brian Augarde was a jazz clarinettist who was a member of the Bletchley Park Jazz Quintet. In this, he and his fellow jazz fans were markedly ahead of their time; popular culture was more about swing. Also at the Park was an American cryptologist called Bob Britton, who had previously worked at the American broadcasting station NBC. He was remembered by fellow cryptanalyst Neil Webster in a letter to his wife: 'He's a shy bloke, terribly attractive in a studious but apparently lackadaisical style. He strums dreamy jazz very pleasantly.'

When, at the end of the war, the remaining Bletchley Park operatives packed up and moved to their new temporary base in north-west London, jazz was coming more to the forefront. Indeed, at one point, the codebreakers there managed to persuade the super-cool pairing of Johnny Dankworth and Cleo Laine to perform for them.

Classical music, with its formal architecture, was one kind of language; the swirling vortex of jazz was another. And yet once more we might see the correlation. Although on first listening certain pieces of improvised jazz might appear unpredictable and even chaotic, nevertheless the flow and feel becomes clear if one listens in the right way. The meanings of jazz are perhaps not quite so obvious as those found in grander, more familiar classical pieces, but here is music that – like modernist poetry – is there to be decoded by the discerning and the intelligent.

So some of the puzzles in this section involve the grammar of musical notation; the codebreakers would have been quite familiar with the possibilities offered up by these symbols.

# 1
## MAJOR TO MINOR

Fit all the listed words into the grid below. Words can read either across or down. All the words containing nine letters have a musical link. There is only one complete answer that can lead you from MAJOR to MINOR.

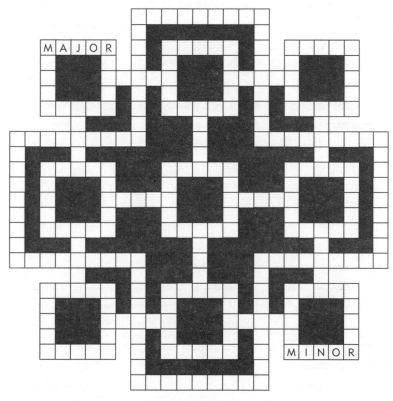

**5 LETTERS**

| | | | | | | | |
|---|---|---|---|---|---|---|---|
| ALBUM | AMONG | APHID | APPLY | BAKER | BLANK | BROKE | CHILL |
| COVER | COWER | DAZED | DRIED | DUKES | ENDED | ENTER | ESSAY |
| FADED | FILTH | FLOOR | GUILD | HEATS | KAYAK | KNOLL | LUCKY |
| MAGIC | MAJOR | MANIA | MANIC | MINOR | OFFER | PATCH | PIANO |
| PROXY | QUIET | QUOTE | RANGE | REBEL | REPLY | ROYAL | SPRIG |
| STRUM | SWEET | TEMPO | TENOR | TEPID | THEME | WASTE | ZEBRA |

**9 LETTERS**

| | | | |
|---|---|---|---|
| CASTANETS | COMPOSERS | CONDUCTOR | CRESCENDO |
| EUPHONIUM | GLISSANDO | HARMONICA | HARMONIUM |
| ORCHESTRA | OVERTURES | RECORDING | SEMIBREVE |

# 2
## COMPOSITION STUDY

There's a keen rivalry at Bletchley to be the best at whatever you set out to be. Playing musical instruments is a popular pastime. Inevitably, there's a desire to be able to play more instruments than anyone else.

David, Jean, Michael and Susan are keen musicians. They can all play the recorder, and everyone except Michael can play the accordion. David is also more than competent playing the mandolin, oboe, trumpet and zither. Jean can play the saxophone, the ukulele and the tuba. Susan can play a euphonium, guitar and lute. Including the recorder, Michael plays three of Susan's instruments. He is the only one to play clarinet and piano. In addition, he plays one other instrument in the list played by David and Jean.

What other instrument can he play?

# 3
## PICTUREDROME

What is the missing letter that has been replaced by a question mark?

1. A  A  A  F  I  N  S  T

2. A  H  O  P  T  T

3. A  A  D  E  G  I  N  O  O  O  P  R  R  S  T

4. A  D  E  F  H  I  O  O  R  T  W  Z  Z

5. E  E  E  I  I  L  M  M  N  O  S  S  T  T  ?

# 4
## PRELUDE

Can you fill in the missing letters on the notes to the solo horn player?

### NOTES TO SOLO HORN PLAYER

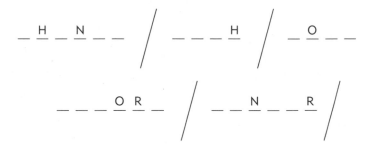

# 5
## QUINTET

Complete the fifth group by replacing the question mark with letters that finish the sequence.

**1.** G   M   V   U   F

**2.** R   K   C   P   Q

**3.** W   X   E   D

**4.** X   V   Y   Q   T   I   X

**5.** M   F   ?   ?

# 6
## ENSEMBLE

Five Bletchley Park musicians have reached the last stage of a music competition. Each individual plays a different musical instrument, performs a work by a different composer and each is placed in a different position by the judges.

When you discover a positive piece of information put a tick in the appropriate square in the grid. Put an X when you discover a piece of negative information. Cross-refer all your information until you can complete the lower grid.

**1.** Phyllis didn't play the clarinet, nor was she placed third.

**2.** One of the male musicians finished in fifth place. This was not Malcolm, who performed a piece by Beethoven.

**3.** Jenny tackled a piece composed by Schubert and played it on her guitar.

**4.** The flautist was placed by the judges directly in front of the young lady playing Handel, who in turn was placed directly above Sheila who played music by Kern.

**5.** A piece by Gershwin was performed by the oboe player.

| | | INSTRUMENT | | | | | COMPOSER | | | | | PLACED | | | | |
|---|---|---|---|---|---|---|---|---|---|---|---|---|---|---|---|---|
| | | CLARINET | FLUTE | GUITAR | OBOE | PIANO | BEETHOVEN | GERSHWIN | HANDEL | KERN | SCHUBERT | FIRST | SECOND | THIRD | FOURTH | FIFTH |
| **NAME** | JENNY | | | | | | | | | | | | | | | |
| | MALCOLM | | | | | | | | | | | | | | | |
| | NEVILLE | | | | | | | | | | | | | | | |
| | PHYLLIS | | | | | | | | | | | | | | | |
| | SHEILA | | | | | | | | | | | | | | | |
| **PLACED** | FIRST | | | | | | | | | | | | | | | |
| | SECOND | | | | | | | | | | | | | | | |
| | THIRD | | | | | | | | | | | | | | | |
| | FOURTH | | | | | | | | | | | | | | | |
| | FIFTH | | | | | | | | | | | | | | | |
| **COMPOSER** | BEETHOVEN | | | | | | | | | | | | | | | |
| | GERSHWIN | | | | | | | | | | | | | | | |
| | HANDEL | | | | | | | | | | | | | | | |
| | KERN | | | | | | | | | | | | | | | |
| | SCHUBERT | | | | | | | | | | | | | | | |

| NAME | INSTRUMENT | COMPOSER | PLACED |
|---|---|---|---|
| | | | |
| | | | |
| | | | |
| | | | |
| | | | |

# 7
## COUNTERPOINT

In music, all notes have a fixed time limit, expressed as a numerical value. This puzzle bears no resemblance to existing musical values, so you do not need a knowledge of musical notation to solve it.

All that you need to know is that the value of each note remains constant, and that no two different-shaped notes can have the same value.

In the square below, the numbers represented by each musical symbol add up vertically and horizontally to give the number at the end of the row or column. First you need to work out the values of each musical symbol.

Now look at the ten triangles labelled A to J below. These ten small triangles fit back into the large empty triangle. Some of them may overlap each other; if there is an overlap, the notes must match. To help you get started, the small triangle with the highest value when all its notes are added together must go at the top of the pointed shape.

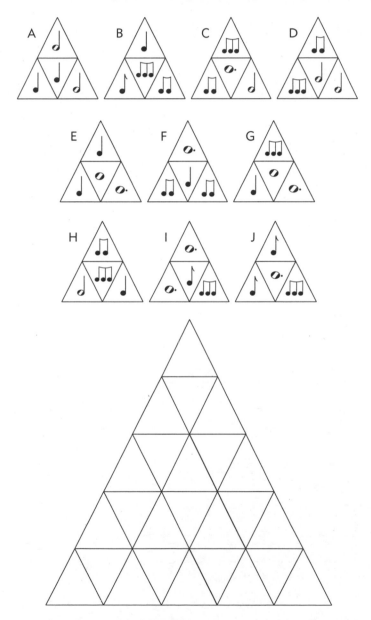

# 8
## RECITATIVE

To whom is the song dedicated?

# 9
## NINTH SYMPHONY

Here are nine symbols used in musical notation. Fill the grid with the symbols, so that each block of 3 x 3 squares contains all nine different symbols, as does each of the nine rows reading across and the nine columns reading down.

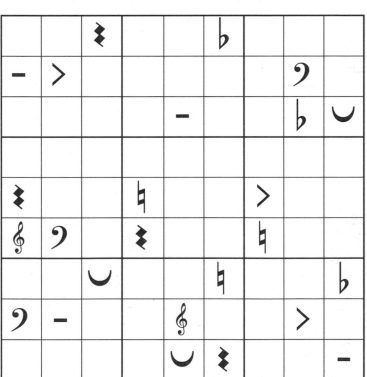

# 10
## SERENADE

**a)** Vera Lynn is inextricably linked with wartime songs. What is the missing word that links with her name in the list below?

ALTO   ANON   OPAL   PONY   RIFT

**b)** How can these words be arranged in columns to name another famous singer from the 1940s?

BORZOI   CHASTE   CHEATS   ENGULF   RECALL   UNITED

# CHAPTER EIGHT

# HIGHLAND REELS AND CROQUET LAWNS

The working life of a codebreaker was horribly sedentary. Their pressurised eight-hour shifts were spent sitting at desks or blackboards, very often in huts with blacked-out windows (even in a small town like Bletchley, the anti-bomber precaution was very much adhered to). There were concerns about the effects that this life might have on health.

In Hut 11, there was an early form of 'Sun-Ray' parlour – that is, a special room with especially strong lights intended to mimic the benefits of sunshine that otherwise would not be seen from week to week. Physical exercise was of terrific importance too, but even the sporty recreations that the codebreakers went in for all had some kind of bearing on the work that they did, and on the mental prowess required for it. So in this section, the puzzles are inspired both by that element of get-up-and-go, and also directly by some of the complex games and dances that the codebreakers favoured.

Sometimes, of course, exercise was about liberation, both for the body and the soul. A strenuous workout could refresh the brain as well as the muscles. Alan Turing found – as have many others after him – that long-distance running was a terrific boon to thinking. Turing (who was twenty-seven when he joined Bletchley) used to cover immense distances along the path of the Grand Union Canal, or across the local, largely flat landscape. A too-fast pace could hinder smooth thought; but a reasonable canter somehow helped to reset the mind. A long-distance run is not only a means of allowing a problem to percolate and stew; at the end of it, the brain is fired up, thanks to the boost in blood circulation.

Turing was so abstracted that he almost accidentally became a seriously proficient runner: he could complete a marathon in around two hours and forty-five minutes, which in those days would have been amply fast enough to qualify for the Olympics.

There were other sports at Bletchley too, and tennis was extremely popular among women and men alike. The codebreakers formed a formal Tennis Society, which was allocated its own small budget for replacement balls and rackets. The secretary of the society received a polite but firm letter from Dunlop in 1942 explaining that the reason for the delay in sending fresh new tennis balls was that supplies were short owing to a small matter of the war.

Tennis involved an explosive force that could be extremely satisfying to unleash after a gruelling night shift. The same went for ping-pong, which was played with noisy avidity. A more measured contest of physicality, intelligence and guile came with fencing; the Bletchley fencing club was popular and contests were fought in a large spare room on the ground floor of the mansion. The quiet intellectual aggression required for unlocking enemy codes found a mirror on the fencing floor when it came to outwitting one's opponents.

Yet not all physical exertion had that quiet dignity. There were other outlets that had a delightful element of sheer childishness. In the winter – and some of the wartime winters were mercilessly ferocious – the lake in front of the mansion would freeze over and the codebreakers would pull on their ice skates. Later in the war, when the Americans arrived, there was keen competition on that ice, in terms of sprints and fancy moves, with the US codebreakers dancing and swerving circles around their British counterparts.

In the bright summers, when there were too many people vying for room on the tennis courts, extemporised games of rounders were played. The distinguished commentator Malcolm Muggeridge – passing through the Park in an intelligence role – looked on with some astonishment as dons he recognised from Oxford and Cambridge cantered around the bases.

Added to all this, there were those who favoured physical exertion with a more geometrical dimension. A mathematician called Leslie Yoxall found that he had an innate talent for the considered (and often malicious) game of croquet. Hoops, opposing balls, a certain level of eagle-eyed ruthlessness in smashing one's opponents out of the way . . . the game comprised all these elements plus of course topography and Newtonian physics. We can imagine that Yoxall saw all the lines, angles and possibilities of repercussion, and was also very handy at calculating weight, mass and force.

Incidentally, we know just how good Yoxall was to become at the game – because while his codebreaking life was cloaked in invisibility, his croquet-playing left a telltale trail. We know, for instance, that he had been quietly persuaded to stay in the new organisation of GCHQ – and we know this not through GCHQ itself but instead through the annals of the Cheltenham Croquet Society. His fellow members had no idea about his day job but he was suitably celebrated as one of their finest players. It was an enthusiasm that Yoxall shared with Hugh Alexander, although Alexander never seemed to reach quite the same local exalted levels.

For those at Bletchley Park who had tired of all the tennis and cricket, there was a new craze to captivate them that had been brought in by the previously mentioned senior codebreaker, Hugh Foss. Foss was an unusually tall man, standing at six foot five, but he was elegant on his feet. And the mad new trend that he introduced to the Park – taking over one of the rooms in the main mansion on a weekly basis – was Highland dancing, or reeling.

Foss himself had been plunged into this colourful swirl of whirling tartan some years previously, when he was labouring on intercepted signals – and examining the earliest form of the Enigma machine – at the then Government Code and Cypher School based in Kensington, west London.

Hugh Foss's Scottish wife Alison had seen how the work left little room either for mental or physical relaxation so one night, in the 1930s, she took Hugh along to a private gathering in a smart house in Chelsea. It was a party, but with a twist: instead of standing about drinking, the guests were instead inveigled to join elaborate Highland dances.

There was something about these dances – possibly the striking blend of fast movement and intense order and regularity – that seized Foss hard. The addiction was instant. We can imagine, in the grey soot of drizzly London, how the greens and blues and reds of the tartan, the bright flashes of jewellery, together with the wailing urgency of the pipes, seemed both powerfully exotic and wonderfully escapist.

Whatever the case, the infatuation was so intense that Foss became an evangelist: he even persuaded fellow codebreaker Alastair Denniston (later to become the Director of Bletchley Park) to come along with his wife to further Chelsea Highland dances. And when all codebreaking was transferred to Bletchley Park in 1939, Foss was not going to let that stop him. Indeed, it would supply him with a new cohort of converts to the art of reels. By this stage, he had started to devise his own.

Among the many eccentricities of the mansion at Bletchley – it had been built by the Leon family in the late nineteenth century and was intended as a grand destination for weekend parties – was a ballroom with a hugely ornate ceiling. Obviously there would be no chance to use real pipers for the music – but with the aid of a gramophone player, it did not take Foss long to set up his Highland Dancing Society. In the summer, the dancing would spill out of the house and onto Bletchley's front lawn, near the lake. And under Foss's expert tutelage, the young enthusiasts learned ever more complex reels.

Among those codebreakers who joined it were Sheila MacKenzie from Aberdeen, and Oliver Lawn from Sheffield. Very soon romance sparked between the two of them as they danced the 'Dashing White Sergeant'. After Bletchley Park, they got married, remaining together for the rest of their lives.

Throughout the war, as Foss grew in experience and seniority, he became one of the key liaison figures between Bletchley Park and the counterpart codebreakers in America. The Americans were beguiled by this russet-haired, gangling figure; because of his enthusiasm for sandal-wearing, he became known as 'Lend-Lease Jesus' (the

'Lend-Lease' part was a satirical reference to the American means of loaning wartime resources to Britain). After the war, when the work of these transatlantic codebreakers was fusing ever tighter together, Foss found himself back in London. And while his daytime hours involved Soviet encryptions, his evenings were once more filled with reels.

In the early 1950s, Foss's highland dancing society featured the young Princess Elizabeth as its patron. He also started a magazine, *The Reel*. He was dissatisfied with the way that Highland dance steps were made into diagrams so he invented a new system, a thing of surpassing complexity, involving symbols and numbers and arrows. Along the way, he devised many new dances: 'Auld Robin Gray', 'Castles in the Air,' 'My Mother's Aye Glowerin' Over Me', and 'The Wee Cooper of Fife' among them. None of the magazine's readers would have guessed that these themselves were a form of code devised by one of the country's finest cryptographers.

There were articles that sought to delve into Highland dancing controversies: particularly tricky moves, or the issue of whether keeping perfectly in step made the dance too much like a military routine or whether looseness would precipitate anarchy on the sprung floor. Foss even provided a bonus with this magazine: cryptic puzzles of his own devising. He simply couldn't help himself.

So the puzzles in this section have a distinctly light-toed feel: a challenge to decode (with an initial key) some complex dance moves. Plus puzzles with an element of croquet combined with Euclidean geometry. Dance and croquet are – rather like snooker – pursuits with the deepest mathematical structures. And when the Bletchley Park codebreakers took to their sprung floors, or the warm close-mown grass of summer, they were seeing these games with very different eyes to their non-codebreaking colleagues.

# 1
## HEAD OVER REELS

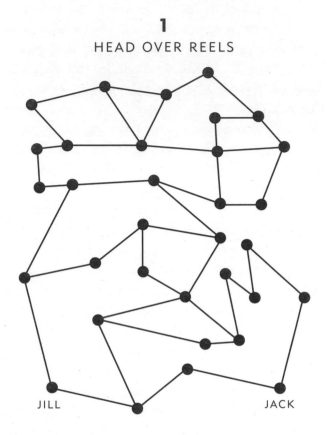

The reel is over. The sketch shows the dancers, represented by black dots in their positions on the floor. The lines indicate the dance moves they have made. Jack is head over reels in love with Jill and wants to move back to her. To do so he must find a route along the lines of dance moves. He must also make an EVEN number of moves and not cross his route.

**a)** What's the least number of moves it will take?

**b)** Jill is not so keen to be reunited with Jack. From their original starting points, what is the largest number of moves (odd or even) that she can make before reaching him?

# 2
## TAKE YOUR PARTNERS

The eighteen words below can each be joined to another word in the list to make a new word. What are the NINE new words? There is only one solution in which each word is partnered once.

| | | |
|---|---|---|
| APACE | BLACK | BOARD |
| CAR | COVE | CUP |
| HOLE | INTER | KEY |
| MAIL | PART | PLAIN |
| RAGE | RIDGE | SEA |
| SON | TIFF | VIEW |

# 3

## THE DEVIOUS DEVISER

Bletchley operative Hamish, in his role as one of the devisers of the Highland Dancing Society, set up by Hugh Foss at Bletchley, was drafting a new set of dance moves, scribbling a few moves and notes on a pad of paper. At the same time he was thinking how he could relate a number-code message to one of the dancers who would be looking at the moves. Looking down at his pad he saw he could do the two things at once. The dance moves could be divided into groups of triangles which just happened to be the number he wanted to transmit. So how many triangles are there?

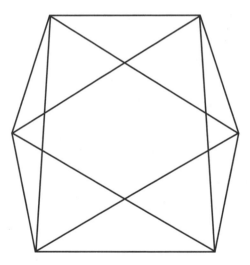

# 4
## STEP TO A REEL

**a)** *Three-couple reel*

The competitive nature of the Bletchley team extended beyond the office to recreational activities too. Here, Sal, who is in charge of the typing pool, has to organise three couples for a three-couple reel competition and she wants them to win. She has chosen:

COUPLE 1: PRUE AND HER PARTNER PETER

COUPLE 2: TERRI AND HER PARTNER ROY

COUPLE 3: ADA AND HER PARTNER ALF

Can you say why Sal has chosen these specific couples?

**a)** *Five-couple reel*

AVA, MAX, TAMMY and TOMMY are on the dance floor. A five-couple reel is about to commence so three more couples must join them. From those waiting on the edge of the dance floor, which six dancers will they be – and why?

AMY    DANNY    EDNA    MATT    MAY    MONA
MONTY    OTTO    TIM    VIV

# 5

## GET IN LINE

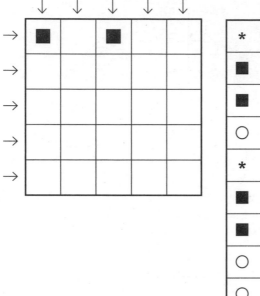

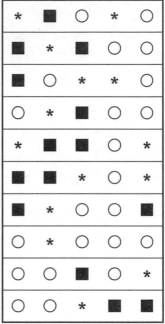

Using a notation system, the positions of dancers on the floor are recorded at the beginning of a dance in a 5 x 5 grid. The organisers have used the following symbols: black square for a gentleman, circle for a lady, with an empty space denoted by a star. They made a note of each row going left to right across, plus a note of each column starting at the top and working down. Unfortunately, these ten pieces of notation have been mixed up, so there is no indication of which are rows or columns or where they should be placed within the 5 x 5 grid.

There are a couple of shapes in place to start you off. Can you fill in the grid using the ten mixed-up lines of notation above?

# 6
## BLETCHLEY RING

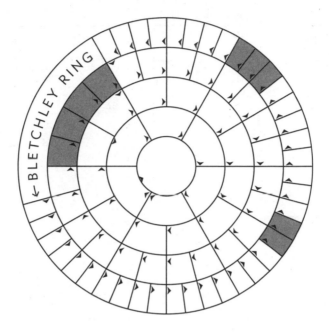

Twenty-two dancers have taken to the floor. Their names link in a spiral, with the end of one name doubling as the beginning of the next – but how many letters overlap? Sometimes it's one, sometimes two, sometimes three or maybe even four! Some spaces are shaded to indicate where names overlap. Can you start in the space next to the large arrow and complete the ring using all the names of the dancers?

ALICE  AMY  ANGELA  ASTRID  BERTRAM
CECIL  DICK  DOUGAL

ELAINE  ELEANOR  HERBERT  JUDITH  LEAH
LIONEL  MYRA

NELLIE  NEVILLE  NORMAN  PHYLLIS  RALPH
SID  THOMAS

# 7
## FOUR TIME

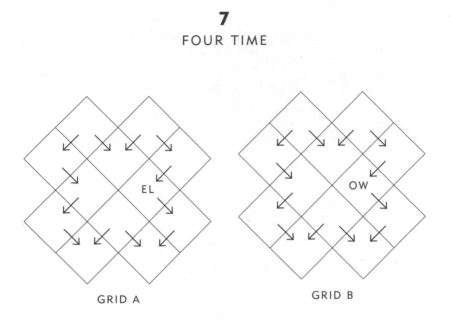

GRID A                              GRID B

Take steps to slot the pairs of letters back into the two grids, so that each grid produces twelve words of four letters each. Start each word by placing two letters in a square and finish it by placing the final two letters in a neighbouring square, following the direction of the arrow. Two letters have already been placed in each grid to start you off.

AM   BU   CE   ED   EK   EL   EX   FT   GS   IT   JI   LL

ON   OW   RA   RE   SE   SH   SO   TE   TO   UP   VE   WE

# 8

## AROUND THE FLOOR

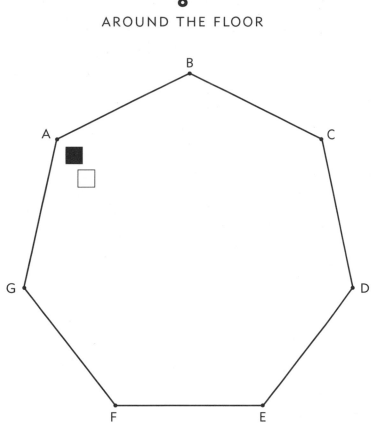

Two dancers are represented by the squares in corner A of the heptagon-shaped dance floor above. The black square is the male dancer and the white square is his lady partner. The gentleman moves around the edges of the floor moving to one corner at a time in a clockwise direction. His lady, on the other hand, moves in an anti-clockwise direction. Her first step is to the next corner but one, and her second step is to the immediately adjacent corner. After that, she continues this 2-1-2-1 pattern around the room. How many moves must each dancer make before they meet up again – and in which corner will this take place?

# 9

## DIAMOND FORMATION

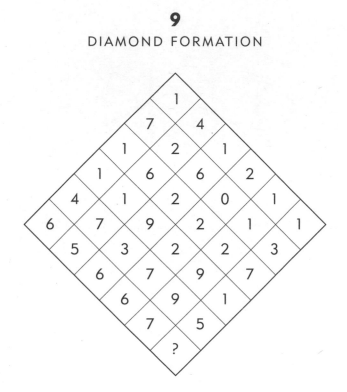

A deviser has been having a fine time writing down his notation for a lively reel. Each number stands for a different set of actions and steps. Not only this, the numbers indicate how an individual should move round the floor. Follow the pattern by moving horizontally, vertically or diagonally from square to square. Each square must be visited once and once only. After deciding your starting place, there is a logical progression to guide you on your path.

What is the number that should replace the question mark at the end of sequence?

# 10
## CROQUET CHALLENGE

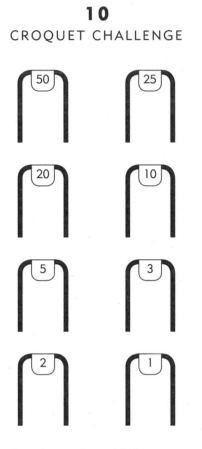

Ideally, croquet is played on a beautifully manicured, perfectly flat piece of turf. However, necessity is the mother of invention, and the inhabitants of Bletchley were well honed in the art of improvisation.

Roger, Sandra and Thomas have made their own croquet challenge. Using the eight hoops they have, a course has been staked out. The hoops have all been given scoring value, based on the difficulty of each location. Hoops on the relatively flat area have low scores. Two hoops, on a tricky slope, carry higher scores of 20 and 25. One hoop, on the edge of a stagnant pond, delights in the name of Old Stinky and carries a scoring value of 50.

They decided to play until each player had run (i.e. scored on) six hoops. Roger made 25 with his first three scores. Coincidentally, his third score was a 3. Thomas had not scored at all when Sandra picked up 2 points.

At the end of the game, 50 had been scored only once; 20, 10 and 1 were scored three times; while 25, 5, 3 and 2 were scored twice.

Surprisingly, despite all passing through different combinations of hoops, all three players ended up with the same score.

Who managed to triumph on Old Stinky?

# CHAPTER NINE

# IT ALL ADDS UP

Let's be honest. For many people, the very sight of a mathematical problem elicits a sort of daunted blankness. And when the maths-averse are faced with a question that involves, for example, the number 47⅓; or the word 'integer'; or the terms 'nodes' and 'medians', complete shutdown is the result.

Maths has traditionally been understood as the domain of so-called 'boffins'. The classic image of Bletchley Park codebreakers, for instance, is that of tousle-headed eccentrics, perhaps a little socially awkward, immersed in abstract depths of equations. Yet the truth was occasionally quite different.

And so the puzzles in this section, although mathematically flavoured, will not require you to possess a first-class degree in the subject: rather, they involve an element of mental gymnastics. An ability to look at numbers and symbols from all angles, even upside down if needs be, to fathom their meanings.

One of the many social assumptions that was itself turned upside down by the codebreakers of Bletchley was that pure mathematics was *Boys' Own* stuff: that the girls could not possibly be expected to understand it. Going further than this, Bletchley Park also underlined the absurdity of a social dichotomy that we still see today: the belief that people who are into the arts don't have a head for numbers.

But while there might be such a thing as a natural aptitude for maths, the story of Bletchley Park is also one of attitude. The codebreakers were faced with problems that could and would be solved. These were problems that in their own way had a curious kind of aesthetic beauty. And for one particular female recruit, the challenge was one she relished. After all, she had already distinguished herself in her field above her male peers.

In 1940, Joan Clarke was at Newnham College Cambridge, and she was studying mathematics. This – at the time – was unusual. Very much more so than now, the subject was almost totally male-dominated. More than this: while women had not too long before finally been granted the privilege of studying at Cambridge, and while they could sit examinations together with their male counterparts, they could not actually hope to gain the degrees awarded to the men. The university authorities were – even by 1940 – not quite ready to go that far.

All this notwithstanding, Joan Clarke – the daughter of a vicar who was brought up among the leafy hills of south London – was a brilliant student. And mathematics was a fast-developing subject at that time. The ever-expanding reach of science – to see out among the stars, to peer deep into the heart of atoms, to fly at unthinkable speeds through the sky – meant that mathematicians had to find new means of accommodating fresh discoveries. This meant anything from formulating theories for calculating the mass and movement of gases in space to the effect of turbulence on wing structures.

This was also a time of great advances in geometry – especially when calculating elastic three-dimensional structures – and in statistics too. In other words, maths was not just an abstract discipline. This was a subject at the very heart of the speedily modernising world.

Joan Clarke had more than an aptitude; in each of her three years of study, she scored a First. This made her what the university termed a 'wrangler', an honour very rarely given to women. Yet still the university would not bestow the more customary official honour of a degree. Despite this, the Cambridge University authorities asked Joan to stay on; she clearly had an enormous amount to contribute to the department. But by this time, the air-raid sirens were wailing.

Early in 1940, Joan received a communication from a former lecturer at Cambridge called Gordon Welchman. They met, and she was swiftly inducted into the world of Bletchley. By June 1940, following the British army's shattering retreat from Dunkirk, she was assigned to Hut 8, alongside Peter Twinn and Alan Turing.

Many recruits to Bletchley found the shift system the trickiest thing to adjust to at first. There were three eight-hour 'watches' (a naval term), the toughest of which was midnight to 8 a.m., when the codebreakers would be expected to work on incoming traffic throughout the night. First of all there was the necessary adjustment to new and uncongenial sleeping patterns; second, there were unexpected digestive problems caused by taking meals at unusual times of day. All these symptoms quickly wore off, though they did not help with the general strain.

But the mathematicians in Hut 8 – like many others around the Park – were young and had a lively sense of humour, which was an unquantifiable asset. And so Joan Clarke found herself not only among intellectual peers, but also in an atmosphere of vivacity. The one photograph that exists of her at the Park, taken towards the end of the war, shows a smiling woman surrounded by droll-looking men.

Joan and Alan Turing immediately found a rapport, not least because he was using a variant of Bayesian probability theory to help make his mighty bombe machines work more effectively, a theory that happened to fascinate her. The two of them talked as intellectual equals. Unlike a great many other codebreakers, who found that Turing had a tendency to soar off into the stratosphere, Joan could not only keep up but could also fire back alternative suggestions and ideas. She was one of the very few people in the world capable of doing this.

She was also one of the few people who could listen to Turing's uniquely infuriating laugh without making a move to leave the room. The recent film drama *The Imitation Game* saw Alan and Joan being portrayed by Benedict Cumberbatch and Keira Knightley: fine actors both, but the film was suffused with melancholy. In fact, away from the mind-contorting grind of the work, both Alan and Joan were high-spirited – amused and amusing.

A lot of the work on Enigma involved both probability and statistical analysis and it required more than rock-hard focus; there was also an element of being able to absorb endless letters and figures and somehow see into a dimension beyond them. One codebreaker later said that the key was being able to hold a problem up and then turn it around, examining it from every dimension.

Mathematics was a language and a system of thought all of its own, and Joan Clarke was highly fluent. She and Alan grew closer; took picnics together; went for long walks in the countryside of Buckinghamshire. Their small talk involved such matters as the Fibonacci sequence – a mathematical quirk often found in nature. The Fibonacci sequence is a series of numbers in which every number (after the first two) is the sum of the preceding two. The pattern can be seen in many natural objects, including pine-cones, pineapples and leaf structures. In the case of pine-cones, the nobbly structure consists of two sets of spirals and these spirals conform to Fibonacci numbers. Both Alan and Joan were fascinated by the outward displays of mathematical complexity in nature.

They got engaged but it was short-lived. Turing confessed to Clarke what he termed his 'homosexual tendencies', but they remained colleagues, and indeed good friends.

While Turing was sent off across the Atlantic in 1943 to help the American effort, Joan Clarke rose in Hut 8, eventually becoming deputy director. After the war, they remained close: Turing working on computers and Clarke – quietly and secretly – continuing her hugely successful codebreaking career.

Joan Clarke was by no means alone in her talent. Another prominent female mathematician who was plucked from academe was Margaret Rock; she worked in the Cottage, the outbuilding next to the main house, with Dilly Knox. Knox always seemed to prefer working with women (Mavis Lever was another of his colleagues). A few sniggering colleagues attributed this to lasciviousness, but it seemed more the case that women very often were much better at the job. Mavis Lever was handed a pencil when she first arrived, and was told by Knox: 'Here, we're breaking machines. Do you want to have a go?'

There were also those for whom the drift into mathematics had seemed to be a question of serendipity, rather than temperament.

At the age of ten, in 1930s London, young Peter Hilton was unfortunately knocked over by a Rolls-Royce. He had to spend some weeks in hospital with his legs in plaster and while he was there, he was supplied with writing material and a blackboard. He passed those long, long days by devising and solving mathematical problems.

A few years later, in 1941, as Hilton was studying at Oxford, Alan Turing and Stuart Milner-Barry sent a letter to Winston Churchill demanding that the Prime Minister give them funding for extra equipment and more particularly extra codebreakers. The funding came; the recruiters once more descended upon Oxford. They were looking particularly for mathematicians who also knew some German. Peter Hilton was practically the only one in his tutorial set who fitted this particular bill.

There were some who did fit the 'mad boffin' archetype exactly though. Among the quirkiest of Bletchley's great many quirky recruits was a young doctor of mathematics called Irving Jack Good. Born Isadore Jacob Gudak (his parents were of Russian/Jewish descent), he was brought up in Hackney in London's East End. He was apparently slow to take to reading but had a zeal for maths from a very young age. He contracted diphtheria when he was nine years old and, as with Peter Hilton, the enforced time spent in bed meant that his firework mind had a chance to dazzle. As he lay there, he brooded on irrational square roots, among other mathematical phenomena.

Good was at Cambridge in the late 1930s (a near contemporary of Alan Turing) and he was studying for his doctorate by the time the war broke out. He was eventually recruited to the Park in 1941, as part of the general effort to draw in more mathematicians. He was allocated to Hut 8, and his eccentric ways immediately made a very bad impression upon his boss Alan Turing.

On his first evening, Good was put on a night shift, sifting through the day's U-boat and battleship encryptions. It must be pointed out in fairness to Good that the huts made for a very poor working environment: blue with pipe and tobacco smoke, freezing in the winter and sweatily hot in the summer. And come the night shift . . .

well, on his debut, Good was found to have lain down and fallen fast asleep on the floor. Not the sort of conduct desirable in wartime.

Sleep became something of a recurring theme: Good very much needed his regular eight hours. But the next time his apparent narcolepsy was commented upon, it was for the purposes of offering congratulation.

A dense, complex theorem – and a potential means into naval Enigma codes – had been preying on Good as he fell asleep one night; but when he awoke, a possible solution had presented itself. Good had quite literally dreamed a means of cracking codes.

Good went on to lecture in mathematics at Manchester, under Professor Max Newman, and by the 1960s, he had taken his terrific expertise in the fields of artificial intelligence and probability theory out to America. In Virginia, where it was possible then to pick one's own car number-plates, he opted for '007 IJG'. Bond's serial number was intended as a wry reference to his own role in wartime espionage.

In the later years of the war, even those not long out of school were picked up by Bletchley's recruitment tractor beam. In Scotland, eighteen-year-old prodigy Sandy Green – who had started at the University of St Andrews two years early, aged sixteen – found himself in the Bletchley spotlight. The teenager was summoned to be what was termed a 'human computor', that is, someone who makes calculations; if that sounds rather robotic, his time at Bletchley was actually the reverse. As well as being terrific experience in its own right, Green met his wife-to-be, Margaret Lord, at the Park. Romance was everywhere, even among the most dishevelled mathematicians.

Twenty-year-old Oliver Lawn, who had just graduated in maths at Cambridge, found the Bletchley induction a little trying. He found it difficult to focus while being shown a captured Enigma machine because, he said, out the window he could see a number of 'nubile young ladies walking around'. But as noted previously, it wasn't long before his head was permanently turned while dancing with Sheila MacKenzie.

All the above, together with other distinguished names like David Rees, helped to shape the mathematical thinking of a generation:

this was a time when topology and geometry and algebra to do with curves and irregular surfaces – what was termed 'rubber sheet topology' – was being explored in greater depth, which in turn went some way towards mapping structures like the double helix.

After the war, many of Bletchley Park's most abstracted boffins either returned to Oxford or followed the great Bletchley guru Professor Max Newman to the University of Manchester, where a whole new world of computing and mathematics was beckoning.

The new developments were exciting, but perhaps mathematics has never been so indispensable as it was during wartime. The three Polish mathematicians who first cracked Enigma and developed the techniques that they handed over to the British codebreakers in that forest outside Warsaw; Turing's vaulting leaps of Bayesian probability that made the bombe machines a practical means of large-scale code-crunching; the efforts of Professor Max Newman and his team in the 'Newmanry' that made it possible to read messages being sent from the desk of Hitler himself; and the mathematical thinking that led to Tommy Flowers creating the first computer, as we shall see in the next chapter, all played their part in changing the course of history.

The puzzles in this section are vintage brainteasers with a mathematical flavour; these particular examples were extremely popular in Edwardian years, published in magazines and books, and many codebreakers (and of course others) will have cut their teeth on such problems. They don't require a doctorate in Bayesian theory but, in their deceptively quaint way, they do give an idea of the sort of elasticity of thinking that was required at Bletchley: the ability to hold both numbers and concepts in one's head is crucial to problem solving.

# 1

## MRS TIMPKINS'S AGE

EDWIN: 'Do you know, when the Timpkinses married eighteen years ago Timpkins was three times as old as his wife, and today he is just twice as old as she?'

ANGELINA: 'Then how old was Mrs Timpkins on the wedding day?'

Can you answer Angelina's question?

# 2

## A TIME PUZZLE

How many minutes is it until six o'clock if fifty minutes ago it was four times as many minutes past three o'clock?

# 3

## DIGITS AND SQUARES

It will be seen in the diagram that we have so arranged the nine digits in a square that the number in the second row is twice that in the first row, and the number in the bottom row three times that in the top row. There are three other ways of arranging the digits so as to produce the same result. Can you find them?

| 1 | 9 | 2 |
|---|---|---|
| 3 | 8 | 4 |
| 5 | 7 | 6 |

# 4

## THE FOUR SEVENS

In the illustration Professor Rackbrane is seen demonstrating one of the little posers which he is accustomed to entertain his class. He believes that by taking his pupils off the beaten tracks he is better able to secure their attention, and to induce original and ingenious methods of thought. He has, it will be seen, just shown how four 5s may be written with simple arithmetical signs so as to represent 100. Every juvenile reader will see at a glance that his example is quite correct. Now, what he wants you to do is this: Arrange four 7s (neither more nor less) with arithmetical signs so that they shall represent 100. If he had said we were to use four 9s we might at once have written 99 + (9 ÷ 9), but the four 7s call for rather more ingenuity. Can you discover the little trick?

# 5

## VISITING THE TOWNS

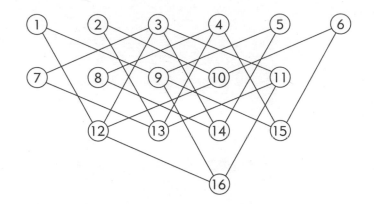

A traveller, starting from town no. 1, wishes to visit every one of the towns once, and once only, going only by roads indicated by straight lines. How many different routes are there from which he can select? Of course, he must end his journey at no. 1, from which he started, and must take no notice of crossroads, but go straight from town to town. This is an absurdly easy puzzle, if you go the right way to work.

# 6

## NEXT-DOOR NEIGHBOURS

There were two families living next door to one another at Tooting Bec – the Jupps and the Simkins. The united ages of the four Jupps amounted to 100 years, and the united ages of the Simkins also amounted to the same. It was found in the case of each family that the sum obtained by adding the squares of each of the children's ages to the square of the mother's age equalled the square of the father's age. In the case of the Jupps, however, Julia was one year older than her brother Joe, whereas Sophy Simkin was two years older than her brother Sammy. What was the age of each of the eight individuals?

# 7

## CURIOUS NUMBERS

The number 48 has this peculiarity, that if you add 1 to it the result is a square number (49, the square of 7), and if you add 1 to its half, you also get a square number (25, the square of 5). Now, there is no limit to the numbers that have this peculiarity, and it is an interesting puzzle to find three more of them – the smallest possible numbers. What are they?

# 8

## THE FARMER AND HIS SHEEP

Farmer Longmore had a curious aptitude for arithmetic and was known in his district as the 'mathematical farmer'. The new vicar was not aware of this fact when, meeting his worthy parishioner one day in the lane, he asked him in the course of a short conversation, 'Now, how many sheep have you altogether?' He was therefore rather surprised at Longmore's answer, which was as follows: 'You can divide my sheep into two different parts, so that the difference between two numbers is the same as the difference between their squares. Maybe, Mr. Parson, you will like to work out the little sum for yourself.'

Can the reader say just how many sheep the farmer had? Supposing he had possessed only twenty sheep, and he divided them into two parts 12 and 8. Now, the difference between 12 and 8 is 4, but the difference between their squares, 144 and 64, is 80. So that will not do, for 4 and 80 are certainly not the same. If you can find numbers that work out correctly, you will know exactly how many sheep Farmer Longmore owned.

# 9

## MRS HOBSON'S HEARTHRUG

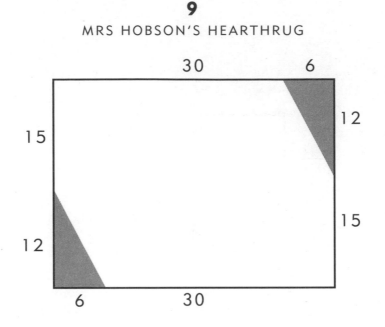

Mrs Hobson's boy had an accident when playing with fire, and burnt two of the corners of a pretty hearthrug. The damaged corners have been cut away, and it now has the appearance and proportions shown in the diagram above. How is Mrs Hobson to cut the rug into the fewest possible pieces that will fit together and form a perfectly square rug? It will be seen that the rug is in proportions 36 x 27 (it does not matter whether we say inches or yards), and each piece cut away measured 12 and 6 on the outside.

# 10
## THE CHOCOLATE SQUARES

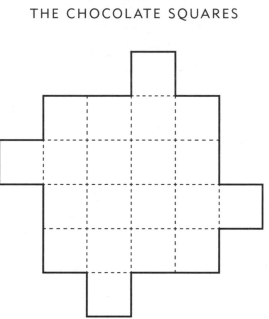

Here is a slab of chocolate. Make a copy of the slab in paper or cardboard and then try to cut it into nine pieces so that they will form four perfect squares all of exactly the same size.

# 11
## THE WIZARD'S CATS

A wizard placed ten cats inside a magic circle as shown in our illustration, and hypnotised them so that they should remain stationary. He then proposed to draw three circles inside the large one, so that no cat could approach another cat without crossing a magic circle. Try to draw the three circles so that every cat has its own enclosure and cannot reach another cat without crossing a line.

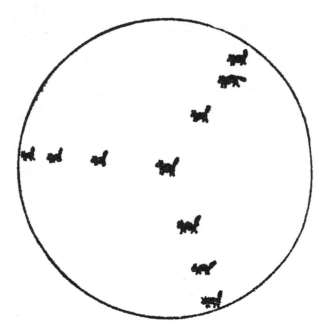

# 12
## THE THREE RAILWAY STATIONS

As I sat in a railway carriage I noticed at the other end of the compartment a worthy squire, whom I knew by sight, engaged in conversation with another passenger, who was evidently a friend of his.

'How far have you to drive to your place from the railway station?' asked the stranger.

'Well,' replied the squire, 'if I get out at Appleford, it is just the same distance as if I go to Bridgefield, another fifteen miles farther on; and if I changed at Appleford and went thirteen miles from there to Carterton, it would still be the same distance. You see, I am equidistant from the three stations, so I get a good choice of trains.'

Now I happened to know that Bridgefield is just fourteen miles from Carterton, so I amused myself in working out the exact distance that the squire had to drive home whichever station he got out at. What was the distance?

# 13

## FARMER WURZEL'S ESTATE

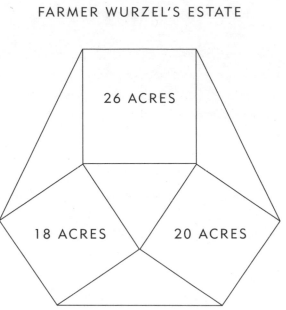

Farmer Wurzel owned the three square fields shown in the annexed plan, containing respectively 18, 20, and 26 acres. In order to get a ring-fence round his property he bought the four intervening triangular fields. The puzzle is to discover what was then the whole area of his estate.

## 14
### THE CRESCENT PUZZLE

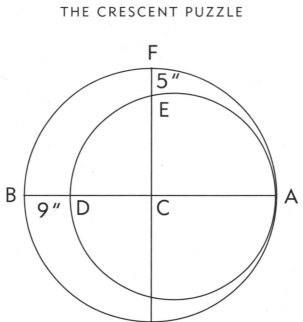

Here is an easy geometrical puzzle. The crescent is formed by two circles, and C is the centre of the larger circle. The width of the crescent between B and D is 9 inches, and between E and F 5 inches. What are the diameters of the two circles?

# 15

## THE DISSECTED CIRCLE

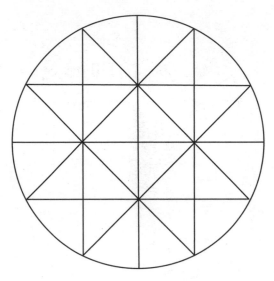

How many continuous strokes, without lifting your pencil from the paper, do you require to draw the design shown in our illustration? Directly you change the direction of your pencil it begins a new stroke. You may go over the same line more than once if you like. It requires just a little care, or you may find yourself beaten by one stroke.

# 16
## THE INDUSTRIOUS BOOKWORM

Our friend Professor Rackbrane is seen in the illustration to be propounding another of his little posers. He is explaining that since he last had occasion to take down those three volumes of a learned book from their place on his shelves, a bookworm has actually bored a hole straight through from the first page to the last. He says that the leaves are together three inches thick in each volume, and that every cover is exactly one-eighth of an inch thick, and he asks how long a tunnel had the industrious worm to bore in preparing his new tube railway. Can you tell him?

# 17
## THE CITY LUNCHEONS

Twelve men connected with a large firm in the City of London sit down to luncheon together every day in the same room. The tables are small ones that only accommodate two persons at the same time. Can you show how these twelve men may lunch together on eleven days in pairs, so that no two of them shall ever sit twice together? We will represent the men by the first twelve letters of the alphabet, and suppose the first day's pairing to be as follows:

(A B) (C D) (E F) (G H) (I J) (K L).

Then give any pairing you like for the next day, say:

(A C) (B D) (E G) (F H) (I K) (J L),

and so on, until you have completed your eleven lines, with no pair ever occurring twice. There are a good many different arrangements possible. Try to find one of them.

# 18
## THE WRONG HATS

'One of the most perplexing things I have come across lately,' said Mr Wilson, 'is this. Eight men had been dining not wisely but too well at a certain London restaurant. They were the last to leave, but not one man was in a condition to identify his own hat. Now, considering that they took their hats at random, what are the chances that every man took a hat that did not belong to him?'

'The first thing,' said Mr Waterson, 'is to see in how many different ways the eight hats could be taken.'

'That is quite easy,' Mr. Stubbs explained.

'Multiply together the numbers, 1, 2, 3, 4, 5, 6, 7, and 8. Let me see – half a minute – yes; there are 40,320 different ways.'

'Now all you've got to do is to see in how many of these cases no man has his own hat,' said Mr Waterson.

'Thank you, I'm not taking any,' said Mr Packhurst. 'I don't envy the man who attempts the task of writing out all those forty-thousand-odd cases and then picking out the one he wants.'

They all agreed that life is not long enough for that sort of amusement; and as nobody saw any other way of getting at the answer, the matter was postponed indefinitely. Can you solve the puzzle?

CHAPTER TEN

# CODEBREAKERS THROUGH THE LOOKING-GLASS

The creator of *Alice in Wonderland* was not just an expert in poetic nonsense; Lewis Carroll (or Charles Dodgson, to use his real name) was also an Oxford mathematician with a taste for symbolic logic and a distaste, in the sunset of the Victorian era, for new-fangled maths theories and practices. Carroll was a great favourite among the codebreakers of Bletchley Park because he used fanciful and comic means of addressing the skill of lateral thinking.

He was a direct influence on Dilly Knox; famously, Knox challenged new recruit Mavis Lever with the apparently simple question, 'Which direction do the hands of a clock go round?' The answer can either be clockwise or anti-clockwise, depending on which side of the clock-face one is standing. The codebreakers could not simply rely on the hard certainties of maths. They had to be inventive about which directions they approached these problems from: back to front if need be.

And so the puzzles in this section have a more fantastical quality. They are drawn directly from Lewis Carroll himself: brainteasers that he had published in magazines and periodicals, each delighting in logical and mathematical riddles that are suffused with inventiveness. These were the very puzzles on which so many of Britain's finest codebreaking minds had been brought up.

The Carroll cult can be traced back to the First World War cryptology efforts. In the dusty Whitehall corridors and offices that made up the department known as 'Room 40' and 'ID25', *Alice's Adventures in Wonderland* was a frequently referenced text, not just by the young Dilly Knox, but also by Frank Birch (who later helped to form GCHQ) and Bletchley director-to-be Alastair Denniston.

Indeed, it formed the core of a codebreakers' Christmas play written by Frank Birch – who as well as being an accomplished cryptologist was also an actor who would later go on to star in films opposite George Cole and Sid James.

The 'Alice' figure in this play was Dilly Knox's fiancée Olive Roddam. After walking down Whitehall and picking up a loose sheet of paper featuring a coded message that begins 'Ballybunion', Olive finds herself whooshed into the looking-glass world of Room 40, where Dilly Knox is a distracted figure – 'the Dodo' – who uses some very Carrollian absurdist lateral thinking to explain why his spectacles are in his tobacco pouch, and his tobacco is in his sandwich box.

There was an accompanying song: 'Peace, Peace, Oh for some Peace! / Miss Roddam says Knox does not please her / When instead of a mat he makes use of her hat / And knocks out his pipe on the geyser!'

Another British codebreaker lampooned in this play was the man who triumphantly decrypted the Zimmerman Telegram – a 1917 German diplomatic cable to Mexico that in effect pulled the United States into the Great War. With this decryption, Nigel de Grey pulled off a cipher feat that changed the course of history. Nonetheless, the slightly built de Grey was cast as 'the Dormouse' and indeed was known by this nickname even up until the 1950s, when he was turning his laser-beam gaze onto the latest Soviet codes.

The codebreakers who were assembled during the First World War tended to be classicists (though Frank Birch was a historian and Nigel de Grey by profession a publisher). They had minds that could range far and wide, however, and it was not only Alice's adventures that prompted a new way of looking at the world; it was also Carroll's approach to lateral-thinking logic problems that helped their own thinking along.

There were currents of deep learning in Alice and her seemingly absurd world and the codebreakers certainly sensed that there was much more to the heroine's adventures than free-range nonsense. Recently, eschewing modern theories to do with psychoanalysis, Melanie Bayley in the *New Scientist* magazine detected a sly satire on abstract maths itself – an angle that would have had tremendous appeal to the Bletchley codebreakers.

Bayley pointed to the *Alice* chapter 'Advice from a Caterpillar', where Alice has shrunk and a mushroom seems to provide the chance to restore her. But this restoration proves madly uneven, with Alice gaining an unwanted extra-long neck. Bayley suggested that this was Carroll's impatience with the growth in abstract maths. His was a world where algebra and its symbols stood for real numbers and real things. But in late nineteenth-century Oxford, this world was increasingly being marginalised; now you could have imaginary numbers – negative numbers – and you could put them into algebraic calculations and produce fascinating results, so long as you followed internal logic.

Bayley argues that *Alice* partly reflected what Carroll saw as mathematical anarchy: Alice can't remember her times table, and the Caterpillar seems perfectly relaxed about this and indeed her constantly changing dimensions. This is an absurd world so why should this instability worry him? The same goes for the apparently insoluble Carollian riddle: 'Why is a raven like a writing desk?'

For master codebreaker Dilly Knox, there was clearly something hugely liberating in finding the internal logic behind seemingly arbitrary statements and, indeed, arbitrary jumbles of letters. His Lewis Carroll fixation and way of thinking continued at Bletchley and – according to Michael Smith – only the women who worked closely with him at the Cottage in Bletchley Park seemed able to see the clear route of his thinking.

One day Knox mystifyingly declared: 'If two cows are crossing the road, there must be a point when there is only one and that is what we must find.' He was referring in an extremely elliptical way to the problem of the Abwehr – or German secret service – Enigma codes. Only Mavis Lever and Phyllida Cross appeared able to follow what he meant. Sadly, his precise meaning has once more fallen into dark obscurity.

Elsewhere, when discussing the moving rotor wheels of the Abwehr Enigma machine, which carried the encoding letters, Knox had observed how sometimes two rotors turned simultaneously and other times all four turned simultaneously. These phenomena he termed Crabs and Lobsters. Crabs were apparently of little use to him. Yet lobsters were.

In another codebreaking method, Mavis and Phyllis were trained to be on the lookout for 'Females' (that is, particular alignments on the hole-punched code-unravelling sheets of card). As with all the other colourful terminology, they were unfazed; indeed, Mavis Lever took pleasure in recounting and explaining Knox's foibles when at last the curtain of secrecy was lifted from Bletchley in the 1980s and 90s.

Funnily enough, Mavis Lever's talent for looking at problems from Carollian angles had been noted before Bletchley Park when she had been working at the Ministry of Economic Warfare. There was a Morse code transcript that referred to a place called 'St Goch'. No such place exists and the meaning of the message could not be fathomed. Miss Lever saw the letters in quite a different way, however; she perceived that the message was referring to Santiago, Chile – 'Stgo Ch'. That was the moment, according to David Lambert (a later academic colleague of hers) when the move to Bletchley Park became a certainty.

Lewis Carroll continued to have a bearing on Mavis Lever's life after she became Mrs Batey and later became a landscape historian. Her mathematician husband Keith took on a senior financial role at Oxford University and while they were there, Mrs Batey was able to explore and write about some of the gardens that had inspired the landscapes of *Alice's Adventures in Wonderland*. A few years later, this now prolific author wrote *Alice's Adventures in Oxford*, dealing with Charles Dodgson's time there.

Alice's creator had some influence over Alan Turing too. A little after the war, Turing organised a treasure hunt for family friends and children. Among the elaborate clues were bottles filled with red liquid (one, 'the libation', smelled terrible, the other, 'the potion', was sweet) and made-up words concealed inside books with fake covers that were hidden on bookshelves.

The offbeat, angled way of looking at things was adopted all over the Park. Bill Tutte's triumph in breaking into the German 'Tunny' codes by hand, using only pencil and paper and two months of deep thought, was one such example, enabling the codebreakers to start reading secret communications straight from Hitler himself.

In the deep winter of 1941, and without even seeing the 'Lorenz' code-generating machine that produced the Tunny traffic, Bill Tutte pulled off the unthinkable. Studying the codes, and the patterns that emerged, he painstakingly visualised the sort of technology that would generate them. Using an amazing fusion of intellect and imagination, he summoned a mental picture of the advanced German encoding machine, and looked deep inside it.

And this vision he was then able to communicate to colleagues, in profound detail; it enabled them to build their own new futuristic code-generating – and code-cracking – machinery in response.

In doing so, the engineers also paid tribute to another of Britain's great masters of the surreal: Heath Robinson. For using Bill Tutte's deductions about Tunny as a jumping-on point, it was also possible to construct even more advanced technology to start chewing through these fresh ciphers: a special contraption that with its maze of pulleys and tapes and pipes and cables looked like a comic caricature.

It was called the 'Heath Robinson' because it resembled one of the preposterously over-complicated creations of this talented humorous illustrator. Heath Robinson's world, depicted in a huge range of cartoons, involved activities such as serving food, pouring wine – even attempting to silence noisy nocturnal cats – with devices and gizmos that ran on countless wheels and pulleys, sometimes with the addition of balloons.

By contrast, Bletchley's Heath Robinson was actually built by a brilliant engineer called Tommy Flowers, and the look of it belied its deadly seriousness. This was an advancing world of valve technology, and photo-electric sensors. There was also a great mass of wheels – plus a specially punched continuous paper tape that was the source of equally continuous exasperation when it kept on snapping.

Flowers learned very quickly from all these difficulties, and the technology that he was to dream up in his laboratory afterwards was in quite a different realm. His next creation – the Colossus – was the machine that ushered in the age of programmable computers.

Lewis Carroll himself would doubtless have been thrilled by the influence he had on the formative minds of the codebreakers. In the 1860s, he had devised a few encryption techniques himself, including one that he called the 'Telegraph Cipher', a moderately tricksy variant on letter transposition. It is likely, then, that Carroll would have fancied himself as a codebreaker at Bletchley Park. Certainly, his appetite for puzzles extended, rather like the example of Hugh Foss, to compiling them. In the case of Carroll, he appeared to do this compulsively. He devised cryptograms for *Vanity Fair*; word progression puzzles (for example, turn 'pig' into 'sty' one letter at a time in four moves) for other journals including *The Lady*; and a whole heap of riddles, acrostics, maths teasers and, of course, challenging logic teasers for friends and the wider public alike.

A number of the puzzles in this section were either thought up by Lewis Carroll or were – in their challenge to make you think laterally – inspired by him. These were the sorts of propositions that delighted and beguiled Dilly Knox and Nigel de Grey and a great host of others who came after them.

# 1

## THE CAPTIVE QUEEN

A captive queen and her son and daughter were shut up in the top room of a very high tower. Outside their window was a pulley with a rope round it, and a basket fastened at each end of the rope of equal weight. They managed to escape with the help of this and a weight they found in the room, quite safely. It would have been dangerous for any of them to come down if they weighed more than 15 lbs more than the contents of the lower basket, for they would do so too quick, and they also managed not to weigh less either.

The one basket coming down would naturally of course draw the other up.

How did they do it?

The queen weighed 195 lbs, daughter 165, son 90, and the weight 75.

# 2

## A GEOMETRICAL PARADOX

The four pieces A, B, C and D, which make up the square of area 8 x 8 = 64 square units, is transformed into a rectangle of apparent area 5 x 13 = 65 square units. Where does the extra square unit come from?

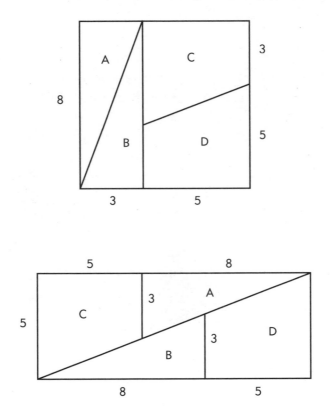

# 3
## THE MONKEY AND WEIGHT PROBLEM

A rope is supposed to be hung over a wheel fixed to the roof of a building; at one end of the rope a weight is fixed, which exactly counterbalances a monkey which is hanging on the other end. Suppose that the monkey begins to climb the rope, what will be the result?

Note: the rope is perfectly flexible and the pulley frictionless.

# 4
## CROSSING THE RIVER

Four gentleman and their wives wanted to cross the river in a boat that would not hold more than two at a time.

The conditions were, that no gentleman must leave his wife on the bank unless with only women or by herself, and also that some one must always bring the boat back.

How did they do it?

# 5
## DOUBLETS

Lewis Carroll called these puzzles 'doublets'. The aim: transform one word into another. The rules: you can change only one letter at a time. The remaining letters must stay in position and all of the words must be in the dictionary.

To get his readers used to the problem, Carroll set a few 'easy' starter puzzles: turn BAT into MAN; TEA into POT; CAR into VAN; and MUM into DAD. Below are a few more that he published in *Vanity Fair* between 1879 and 1880.

Send JOE to ANN
Change TILES for SLATE
Pluck ACORN from STALK
HOAX a FOOL
Bring JACK to JILL
Serve COFFEE after DINNER
Row BOAT with OARS
Change NOUN to VERB
Bring SHIP into DOCK
PLANT BEANS
Raise UNIT to FOUR
Prove LIES to be TRUE
Turn HORSE out to GRASS
OPEN GATE
CRY OUT
Send BOWLER to WICKET

# 6
## NAMES IN POEMS

The poem below was written by Lewis Carroll accompanying a present of a book called *Holiday House*, for the three young daughters of Dean Liddell. The poem contains not only the title of Catherine Sinclair's book but also, hidden within, the names of the three children. Those familiar with the story of Lewis Carroll's life will have a head start with those names!

Little maidens, when you look
On this little story-book,
Reading with attentive eye
Its enticing history,
Never think that hours of play
Are your only HOLIDAY,
And that in a HOUSE of joy
Lessons serve but to annoy:
If in any HOUSE you find
Children of a gentle mind,
Each the others pleasing ever –
Each the others vexing never –
Daily work and pastime daily
In their order taking gaily –
Then be very sure that they
Have a life of HOLIDAY.

Another poem that Lewis Carroll wrote as a riddle contains the name of another of his young correspondents. At first sight, this problem is slightly more intractable than the last . . .

> Beloved Pupil! Tamed by thee,
>     Addish=,  Subtrac=, Multiplica=tion,
> Division, Fractions, Rule of Three,
>     Attest thy deft manipulation!
>
> Then onward! Let the voice of Fame
>     From Age to Age repeat thy  story,
> Till thou hast won thyself a name
>     Exceeding even Euclid's glory.

# 7

## FEEDING THE CAT

> Three sisters at breakfast were feeding the cat,
> The first gave it sole – Puss was grateful for that:
>     The next gave it salmon – which Puss thought a treat:
> The third gave it herring – which Puss wouldn't eat.
>         (Explain the conduct of the cat.)

# 8

## TWO TUMBLERS

Take two tumblers, one of which contains 50 spoonfuls of pure brandy and the other 50 spoonfuls of pure water. Take from the first of these one spoonful of brandy and transfer it without spilling into the second tumbler and stir it up. Then take a spoonful of the mixture and transfer it back without spilling to the first tumbler.

If you consider the whole transaction, has more brandy been transferred from the first tumbler to the second, or more water from the second to the first?

# 9
## ELIGIBLE APARTMENTS

A tutor and his two scholars, Hugh and Lambert, are looking for lodgings. They come across a square in the town that has four houses displaying cards which say 'Eligible Apartments'. However, only single rooms are to be had. There are 20 houses on each side of the square, the doors of which divide the side into 21 equal parts. The houses with the available lodgings are at numbers 9, 25, 52 and 73. The tutor decides to make one of the rooms a 'day-room' and take the rest as bedrooms. He sets this problem for his scholars:

'One day-room and three bed-rooms . . . We will take as our day-room the one that gives us the least walking to do to get to it.'

'Must we walk from door to door, and count the steps?' said Lambert.

'No, no! Figure it out, my boys, figure it out!'

Hence, with the provision that it is possible to cross the square directly from door to door, which house will be used for the day-room?

# 10
## WHO'S COMING TO DINNER?

The Governor – of-what-you-may-call-it – wants to give a *very* small dinner-party, and he means to ask his father's brother-in-law, his brother's father-in-law, his father-in-law's brother, and his brother in-law's father: and we're to guess how many guests there will be.

What are the minimum number of guests at the dinner party?

# CHAPTER ELEVEN

# GOOD, SMART, COMMON SENSE

For the Honourable Sarah Baring, the invitation to work at Bletchley Park had come about partly through opera.

As an upper-class society girl, she had initially found herself working for the war effort making aeroplane parts at the Slough Industrial Estate, the novelty of which had soon worn off. Through family connections, the Honourable Sarah managed to get an interview with the Foreign Office. She was asked if she knew any German and Italian. German wasn't a problem – she was fluent from time spent there in the 1930s. Italian: what she did know came from *La Traviata* but she wasn't going to let that stop her. The bluff worked. She soon found herself on a train from London Euston to the north of Buckinghamshire with a suitcase and a few prized records.

And so the puzzles in this section are to do with the uncelebrated virtues of common sense, allied with quick wits. A great many Bletchley recruits were not remotely academic. Although they had had terrific basic educations, the debutantes and Wrens had very often left school before sixth form.

Perhaps this is why a few of them later referred to Bletchley as 'their university'. But even if you weren't codebreaking, you were still required to work with lightning speed and mental sharpness at all times, and always against the clock.

Some things never change. Alastair Denniston, the director of Bletchley Park, had written himself to the Foreign Office in the early stages of the war. When it came to recruits from both the Wrens and the Auxiliary Territorial Service (ATS), he said, he would prefer if they did not send him 'too many of the cook and messenger type'. So it was that when women volunteered for the Wrens, there was not only a test but also a questionnaire that probed their interests. The authorities were also asked to be alert for 'a high standard of mental agility.'

A great number of the Wrens were destined to work with the bombe machines. While it was not necessary for them to have specifically high skills in advanced mathematical theory, or indeed hugely in-depth knowledge of German or Italian, they were required to be able to respond quickly to exacting circumstances. The machines themselves, while being marvels, were nonetheless very difficult to deal with when they broke down. Wrens were required – even during the 2 a.m. shifts – to be able to fix temperamental bombes with tweezers or indeed anything else that came to hand.

As reported by Christopher Grey in his book *Decoding Organization*, there was a later survey of the Wrens who had worked on the Colossus machines, which were extraordinarily complex pieces of technology. More Wrens in this area had qualifications – but still a very large number did not. 'Twenty-one per cent had Higher Certificate, 9 per cent had been to a university, 22 per cent had had some after-school training, and 28 per cent had had previous paid employment,' wrote Grey. 'None had studied mathematics at university.'

It has also been noted by Grey that many of the young women siphoned through to Bletchley had had unusually superior primary and secondary educations, and came from solidly middle-class backgrounds (the same tended to be true of the WAAFs from the Women's Auxiliary Air Force, whereas the ATS attracted more women from a working-class and less educationally privileged background).

Wren Ruth Bourne – a young woman from Birmingham who had devoured spy thrillers in her youth and so guessed very quickly what the establishment of Bletchley was for – had had further education in Switzerland. Barbara Moor had attended grammar school and then went to college thereafter. Jean Valentine, meanwhile, had been taught at Perth Academy, a school with a towering reputation (indeed, the Scottish state education system generally was for many decades one of the great wonders of the world). The daughter of a prominent local Perth businessman, Jean left school at sixteen, which was perfectly common for women at the time. But the school had already given her an all-round grounding that might be comparable to A-level or even first-year degree level today.

Another Bletchley veteran, Jean Millar, talking as part of a special GCHQ event to celebrate women's history, recalled that she had just taken her solicitor's intermediate exam in 1943 when she volunteered for the Wrens. She found herself posted to the out-station Eastcote, which is in the north-west of London. Here was an array of bombe machines, divided into bays, each bay dedicated to an Allied country. Round the clock, the machines crunched through codes that had been intercepted and sent from all over the world.

The challenge here for Jean Millar was to apply her intelligence to something wholly, completely new. This was no time for abstractions; instead, she and her fellow Wrens had to be intensely practical as well as nimble-witted.

She remembered that in-depth technological expertise was not necessary; in the case of machines breaking down completely, there were special teams of engineers from the British Tabulating Machine Company. That said, however, it was the job of the Wrens, working with fine brushes, to make sure that the rotating drums and other features were maintained in good order and that the machines kept moving.

Others remembered that the strain of tending to the bombes – combined with the incessant 'tickety-clicking' noise and the very fine, almost invisible mists and sprays of oil that they generated – could sometimes get too much. The knowledge of the importance of the work, together with the almost hallucinatory monotony, induced occasional breakdowns.

And the cure for a breakdown? One young woman was prescribed a couple of days in bed, with a jug of water. Anne Hamilton-Grace took this one stage further, replacing the water with a jug of orange juice and gin. However, the point was that there was sympathy and concern: the Bletchley authorities were keenly aware of how debilitating the work could be.

And they were careful about the welfare of the Wrens. Given the intense secrecy of the work, it was in Bletchley's interests to ensure that they were not forced to crash out of the secret war.

There were isolated cases of accidental disclosure: a former Wren who went on to work in London let slip about some of the machinery that she had been working with. What was remarkable was that Bletchley's security precautions – the said young woman was contacted and reminded sternly of the Official Secrets Act – stretched out so far from the Park itself.

Despite the grinding nature of the work, what these Wrens needed above all was the ability to extemporise. This was perhaps more on display with the operation of the Colossus machines at Bletchley. With the innovative use of valves, these computers were fearsomely complex. They also generated a great deal of heat.

One Wren remembered how, in the middle of the night, an electric component of the machine flashed just as she was discreetly about to reapply some lipstick. There was a moment of dazed confusion after this thunder-flash; then the Wren's colleague screamed. It looked as though her friend's throat had been cut: there was a bright red line across her neck. It was in fact a line of lipstick.

In another electrical incident, a Wren received an electric shock when touching a keyboard. The laconic engineer's report read: 'Machine OK, operator earthed.'

But the oppressive heat of the machines could also be useful. It was rumoured that during those night shifts, resourceful Wren operators took the opportunity to dry their underwear.

Some Wren officers based outside of the Park were not as sensitive as the Bletchley Directorate when it came to health. Clearly not appreciating just how hard the Colossus and bombe operators were working, they made some women perform an hour's drill after or before shifts. This was obviously madness; the women in question swiftly became exhausted and the authorities had to intervene. The officers in question made the gracious concession of excusing the Wrens the two-mile march to church on Sunday.

For some Wrens, the war was going to introduce them to a wider, more dangerous world than the secret out-stations in the Home Counties. Jean Valentine was nineteen years old when one day she saw her name had gone up on a noticeboard at Bletchley along with a few others.

She was told that she had been selected to be sent abroad for codebreaking duties, but the authorities were not at liberty at that stage to say where. All they required was that Jean seek permission from her father, because she was under the age of twenty-one, the then legal age of majority. Jean was an only child and was sure that her father would be horrified by the idea of the posting. He was not. He gave full permission, telling Jean that in war, everyone had to do their duty.

There was a six-week voyage through U-boat-infested waters and then, for Jean, the first sight of a new realm that would change the course of her life. She and her fellow volunteers were in Colombo, Ceylon. It is difficult to imagine a starker contrast to the sombre grey stone and sober hills of Perth. She gazed at a new world of rich colour and overwhelming scent.

She was there to work on Japanese codes. And she did so in an altogether more attractive kind of wooden hut – slatted bamboo, no blackout blinds – where in the middle of the night shift, she would be shooing away vast insects that had come in to inspect her work.

In off-duty hours, Jean and her friends would travel into the hills to the tea plantations, gazing upon a British empire that in 1945 looked absolutely immoveable. But the wider point is this: Wrens and WAAFs and ATS women seconded into the secret world had a capacity for absorbing novelty, and indeed approaching it with relish.

After all, if someone had told Jean Valentine a year previously that she would be deciphering Japanese weather reports, she would surely have been bemused. And the same went for all those women operating the bombe machines and the Colossi. They were doing something that no one else in the world was doing. They were there at the gates of the future, being given an extraordinary sneak preview. They didn't have to be experts in the new science of programmable computing. But they did have to have an appetite for taking on fresh and wholly unknown challenges.

Indeed, admiring codebreakers looked on throughout 1944 and 1945 as the Wren Colossus operators not only became brilliantly proficient at arranging the machine settings and adjusting the tapes as they ran through, but in essence became themselves among the very first computer programmers.

For the time, it was a relatively emancipated set-up (aside from the issue of wages – women in any capacity always got paid less). Bright-spark Wrens worked alongside young Post Office technicians and languid codebreakers who seemed happy to let the women do the heavy lifting with the computer technology.

And unlike the bombe operators, the Wrens who were working the Colossi were told regularly that the work they were doing was having a huge impact on the war. The reason the authorities had previously held back was the all-encompassing adherence to secrecy, leaving Wrens with little if any idea where the codes were going, and whether all those night shifts were making any difference.

As the war progressed, the monthly briefings for Colossus were still sparse on detail but they had two effects: that of boosting morale, and also boosting intellectual curiosity about the material that the women were handling.

That youthful atmosphere could occasionally prove a strain for older codebreakers though. As Christmas 1944 loomed at Bletchley, there was one night when a couple of the Post Office engineers had stopped for a gossip in the corridor.

A Wren approached, and as she did so, one of the young men pulled a sprig of mistletoe out of his pocket and puckered up. The Wren shrieked and ran away down the corridor. It was at this point that an office door opened to reveal the furious head of section, Professor Max Newman, who was trying to focus on an especially abstruse problem.

On the whole, though, sexual harassment seemed relatively rare. Mutually consenting romance, on the other hand, was rife. Although the Wrens worked extraordinarily hard, they also managed to find time for extra-curricular diversion – and the best means of facilitating diversion was through dances.

Some Wrens were billeted at a nearby stately home – Crawley Grange – which dated back to the fifteenth century. As well as being thick with history (it was once owned by Thomas Wolsey), the house also had a ballroom. The Wrens who lived there thought it would be criminal not to use it. And the dances they hosted were very popular with the codebreakers.

There was one other factor that unified Wrens and the most abstract boffins alike, and that was a passion for the game of bridge. This card game for four people (two opposing teams of two) is, aside from anything else, notorious for generating nuclear levels of ill-will. It is also very much a contest for the sharp-witted. It was enjoyed by Wrens billeted in the marvellously grand surrounds of Woburn Abbey and it was also played with ferocious competitiveness by codebreakers such as Rolf Noskwith and Asa Briggs.

The puzzles in this section reflect not abstruse intellect, but rather a sort of boisterous lively intelligence that the Bletchley recruiters were looking for in the Wrens. There are quick-fire rounds of word and number challenges, which you should aim to complete as quickly as possible, designed not to measure intelligence as such, but rather to assess accuracy of response under pressure.

# 1
## WHERE AM I?

Here are clues to a location. Where are you?

**a)**  FACE

**b)**  A RICE RAG

**c)**  REPORT

**d)**  REAR RIB

**e)**  I USE CATS

**f)**  YELL ROT

**g)**  PRAM LOFT

**h)**  EMIT BLEAT

# 2
## PICK UP STICKS

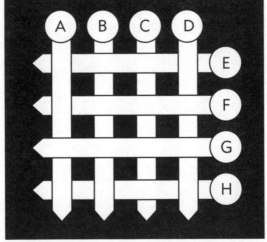

Take off the sticks one at a time so that you are always taking the top one of the pile. In what order do you take them off?

# 3
## CLOTHING COUPONS

Complete the words below by slotting in the name of an item of clothing.

**a)** P A R _ _ _ S

**b)** E S _ _ _ _ D

**c)** W _ _ _ E V E R

**d)** R E _ _ _ _ A N C E

**e)** U N _ _ _ _ A B I L I T Y

**f)** I N _ _ _ _ I T U R E

**g)** R E _ _ _ B I S H M E N T

**h)** I M _ _ _ E D

# 4

## TON UP

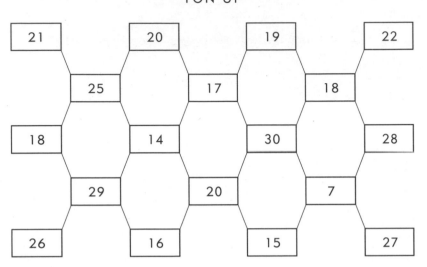

Starting at any number on the top row, move through boxes that are linked to end on the bottom row. The numbers on the way must have a combined total of exactly 100.

Which route do you take?

# 5
## ODD ONE OUT

In each group there is an odd one out. Which is it and why?

**a)** CAROLINA, GEORGIA, LUCIA, VIRGINIA

**b)** BLUNDER, CARP, FLOUNDER, SKATE

**c)** ARROW, CIRCLE, SQUARE, TAP

**d)** EXETER, LINCOLN, PEMBROKE, WINCHESTER

**e)** CHESHIRE, CHICHESTER, GLOUCESTER, LANCASHIRE

**f)** ALES, CARE, HALL, WOOL

# 6
## CREATURE CALCULATIONS

B A T = 8

B O A R = 14

C A T = 9

C R A B = 17

R A T = 7

Every letter has a different value. What number does a COBRA equal?

# 7
## LINK UP

Radio and telephone operators were vital links during World War II. Here you need to link a three-letter word in the left-hand column to a three-letter word in the right-hand column to create a new six-letter word.

| | |
|---|---|
| ANT | TON |
| ASP | RAY |
| BAR | HOD |
| BET | SON |
| COT | ALE |
| DAM | ICE |
| EAR | IRE |
| FIN | ATE |
| HUM | PET |
| LEG | HEM |
| MET | HER |
| OFF | END |
| PAL | OUR |
| PUP | THY |
| WAS | ROW |

# 8
## MANY HAPPY RETURNS

Ron, Steven and Terry are talking about birthdays. They discover that the combined age of the three men and their three wives comes to exactly 150 years. Steven's wife is one year older than he is, while Terry's wife is two years older than Terry. Ron is twice as old as his wife. She is the same age as both Steven and Terry.

How old is Ron?

# 9

## GOING TO THE PICTURES

| O | B | T | R | U | D | E |
|---|---|---|---|---|---|---|
| R | E | G | I | O | N | S |
| B | L | A | S | T | E | D |
| A | D | H | E | R | E | D |
| T | O | P | S | I | D | E |
| T | R | O | O | P | E | D |
| E | N | L | A | R | G | E |

| I | N | T | E | R | I | M |
|---|---|---|---|---|---|---|
| B | O | A | T | C | A | R |
| C | A | S | T | E | R | S |
| C | H | O | R | A | L | S |
| U | N | C | O | A | T | S |
| H | E | C | T | A | R | E |
| T | E | N | S | I | O | N |

The latest film releases from either side of the Atlantic were a major source of entertainment for the Bletchley Park codebreakers. Spin the letters in each left-hand square and slot a new seven-letter word reading across in each grid on the right. When you have finished, the shaded letters in Grid A will reveal a popular actor of the 1940s and the shaded letters in Grid B will tell you where he was bound in 1942.

# 10
## ROTATION

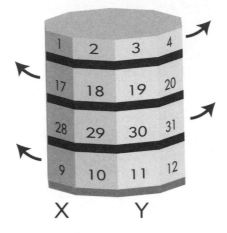

X   Y

The four bands on this drum can move in different directions. The top band rotates in an anti-clockwise direction, as does the third band. The second and fourth bands both rotate in a clockwise direction. Each band contains eight numbers and the number sequence carries on round the drum. The column marked X shows the lowest number featured on each band. Will the total of numbers shown at column Y be greater or less after FIVE rotations of each band?

# 11
## MIDDLE DISTANCE

Two clues, two answers. In the second answer the middle letter has moved further down the alphabet compared to the first answer, e.g. CHASE and CHOSE.

a) DIFFIDENT * CUNNING

b) HEARTBEAT * FUNDS

c) PERFORMANCE * DISCIPLE

d) BEARD * TRIP

e) PARIAH * SURVIVE

f) SPACE * COST

# 12
## VOWEL PLAY

All's fair in love and cryptology! These sentences have had certain letters changed. Try to work out the messages. Vowel play cannot be ruled out!

a) W ND T B NRR BFR W R SF T B SN

b) WI ERI RIEDY END WEOTONG, ERI YUA?

c) THO MURI WA ULOBARETI EAR MOINS IF CAMMENOCUTEEN, THI LASS WU CIMMONACOTI

# 13
## POWER OF THREE

Complete the words by using the same three-letter word in each group.

**a)** G _ _ _ A N T
S Q U _ _ _ Y
R E C _ _ _

**b)** C A _ _ _ A L
J U _ _ _ E R
D E S _ _ _ E

**c)** O C _ _ _ U S
I S O _ _ _ E
A U _ _ _ S Y

**d)** M O _ _ _ T U M
C O M _ _ _ T
P I _ _ _ T O

**e)** A E _ _ _ I C
M I C _ _ _ E
P _ _ _ L E M

# 14
## DAYS

While not on duty on a very wet weekend, Sue starts scribbling on a pad. She notes that the words SUNDAY, TUESDAY and WEDNESDAY are made up from nine different letters of the alphabet. She gives each letter a numerical value from 1 to 9. The numbers in SUNDAY total 28, as do the numbers in TUESDAY.

WEDNESDAY has a far bigger total, 43. DAY itself has a total of 6. No two different letters have the same value. What will be the total of WET DAYS and what is the total of letters in the name SUE?

# 15
## DOUBLE COMBINATION

In the lines of letters below the same combination of letters begins and completes each word.

**a)** _ _ I _ _

**b)** _ _ G I B _ _

**c)** _ _ A L G _ _

**d)** _ _ I R T I E _ _

**e)** _ _ O C K I _ _

**f)** _ _ M P L A _ _

# 16
## SEEING IS BELIEVING

0 APPEARS ELEVEN TIMES.

2 APPEARS TWENTY TIMES.

3 APPEARS TWENTY TIMES.

4 APPEARS TWENTY TIMES.

5 APPEARS TWENTY TIMES.

6 APPEARS TWENTY TIMES.

7 APPEARS TWENTY TIMES.

8 APPEARS TWENTY TIMES.

9 APPEARS TWENTY TIMES.

There is nothing top secret or obscure about the list in which all the above things occur. How many times would the number 1 appear?

# 17

## ALL CHANGE

Whist was a popular card game among the crews at Bletchley. Altering one letter at a time, change the word WHIST into CREWS, making a new word each time you do.

W H I S T

– – – – –

– – – – –

– – – – –

– – – – –

C R E W S

It was a dream come true for many of the Wrens to be stationed at Bletchley, where working round the clock and to tight deadlines was key. Altering one letter at a time, change the word CLOCK into DREAM, making a new word each time you do. See if you can increase your solving time compared to the first challenge!

C L O C K

– – – – –

– – – – –

– – – – –

– – – – –

D R E A M

# 18
## SUM IT UP

**a)** Shapes have taken the place of some numbers in this sum. All the numbers are below ten and no symbol can be the same as a given number. The four digits on the top row when added together produce a smaller total than the four digits on the second row when added together. Can you solve the sum?

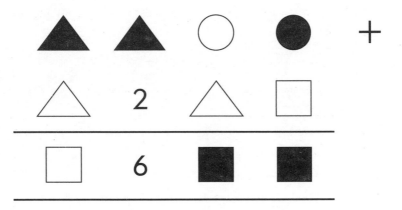

**b)** The following sums do work. Is there a trick? You bet there is!

FIVE × EIGHT = FIVE

SIX – SEVEN = FIVE

FIVE + NINE = SEVEN

# 19
## WORD CHAIN

Find the four-letter answers to the clues in each section. They work as a chain with the last two letters of one word starting the next.

**a)** Develop, Was in debt, Modify, Irritate, Cut, Frank, Concludes

**b)** Cipher, Bureau, Slide, Inspiration, Orient, Stride, Heroic

**c)** Pain, Beneficiary, Metal, Sole, Musical instrument, Harvest, Pinnacle

**d)** Flightless bird, Spouse, Festival, Rip, Dry, Lazy, Page

**e)** Nought, Flower, Insignia, Singing voice, Roman robe, Quarry, Repair

# 20
## CIRCULAR TOUR

**a)**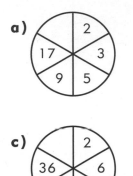

**b)**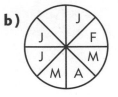

**c)**

**d)**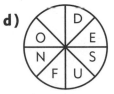

**e)**

**f)**

Complete the circles.

# CONCLUSION

Through the puzzles included in this book we hope that you can begin to understand the wide range of minds – and approaches – that were exploited so brilliantly at Bletchley Park. For whether they were working at nightmare speed during the extraordinary drama of D-Day in June 1944 – Bletchley Park's decrypts being fed back to Churchill constantly to enable him to see how the Germans were responding – or taking the longer-term approach to devise methodologies into cracking Enigma, everyone at Bletchley had to work not just with vigour but also a high-spirited alertness.

It is not too much to say that throughout those dark years the destiny of Europe was being shaped by the amazing puzzle-solving capacities of the extraordinary Bletchley Park veterans. The astounding thing now is that under that unthinkable pressure, the codebreakers tackled each fresh day, each fresh encryption, exactly as though they were *Times* crosswords, or delightfully fiendish conundrums. That love of puzzles – the amused determination not to be bettered by the person devising the problem – kept these young people not only constantly eager and hungry to smash the Nazi codes, but to do so in a way that helped protect their sanity.

One of the reasons the restored Bletchley Park Museum – with its historically accurate huts and grounds – is so popular today is that visitors are attracted by this central idea: that the people recruited for this extraordinary intellectual hothouse were, like them, quite simply puzzle addicts at heart.

# BIBLIOGRAPHY

Alexander, Conel Hugh O'Donel, *Alexander on Chess* (Pitman, 1974)

Atkinson, George, *Chess and Machine Intuition* (University of Chicago, 1993)

Dudeney, Henry Ernest, *Amusements in Mathematics* (Thomas Nelson and Sons, Ltd., 1917)

Glyn-Jones, Anne, *Morse Code Wrens of Station X: Bletchley's Outer Circle* (Amphora, 2017)

Grey, Christopher, *Decoding Organization: Bletchley Park, Codebreaking and Organization Studies* (Cambridge University Press, 2012)

Hinsley, Sir F. H. (ed.), *Codebreakers: The Inside Story of Bletchley Park* (Oxford University Press, 1992)

Pearson, Joss, *Neil Webster's Cribs For Victory: The Untold Story of Bletchley Park's Secret Room* (Polperro, 2011)

Wakeling, Edward, *Rediscovered Lewis Carroll Problems* (Dover, 1995)

# ENDNOTES

CHAPTER ONE: THE WORLD'S MOST FAMOUS
CROSSWORD

**'I received a letter marked "confidential"':** Tom Chivers, 'Could
You Have Been a Codebreaker at Bletchley Park?', *Daily Telegraph*,
10 October 2014

**'I got a communication from the Signal Intelligence Service':**
National Security Agency online archives, Virginia

**'One Bletchley codebreaker, thinking back over his time at the
Park':** Keith Batey, Interviewed by the author, March 2009

**'They were certainly more diverse':** Phil McNeill, 'Can You Solve
the *Telegraph*'s D-Day Crossword?', *Daily Telegraph*, 2 May 2014

CHAPTER TWO: THE MORSE MASTERMINDS

**'Every day we ditted and dahed':** Anne Glyn-Jones, *Morse Code Wrens
of Station X*, 2017

CHAPTER THREE: THE ENIGMA CONNECTION

**'An oik is always an oik':** Keith Batey, Interviewed by the author,
2009

CHAPTER FIVE: THE CHESSBOARD WAR

**'My experience . . . is that it is very difficult to lose at chess with good grace':** Conel Hugh O'Donel Alexander, *Alexander on Chess*, 1974

**'Denniston understood that chess players tend to make good cryptographers':** George Atkinson, *Chess and Machine Intuition*, 1993

CHAPTER SIX: THE CODES FROM THE MUMMY'S TOMB

**'In April 1940, about the end of the phoney war':** Sir F. H. Hinsley (ed.), *Codebreakers: The Inside Story of Bletchley Park*, 1992

**'From 1912 to 1919 . . . Voynich attempted to interest scholars':** National Security Agency online archives, Virginia

**'This book, bequeathed to me by an intimate friend'** Eamon Duffy, 'Secret Knowledge – or a Hoax?', *New York Review of Books*, 20 April 2011

**'When the time comes . . . I will prove to the world':** Ibid.

**'The world of American cryptology':** National Security Agency online archives, Virginia

**'My analysis . . . languages simply do not behave in this way':** Ibid.

**'To the best of my knowledge':** Ibid.

CHAPTER SEVEN: MUSIC, MAESTROS!

**'I played in the Chamber Music Group':** http://www.discovermil-tonkeynes.co.uk/uploads/1/0/3/9/10393340/15g.pdf

**'He's a shy bloke':** Joss Pearson, *Neil Webster's Cribs For Victory: The Untold Story of Bletchley Park's Secret Room*, 2011

CHAPTER NINE: IT ALL ADDS UP

**'nubile young ladies walking around':** Oliver Lawn, Interviewed by the author, February 2009

CHAPTER TEN: CODEBREAKERS THROUGH THE LOOKING-GLASS

**'Peace, Peace, Oh for some Peace! . . . And knocks out his pipe on the geyser!':** Mavis Batey, *Dilly: The Man Who Broke Enigmas*, 2017
**'Recently, eschewing modern theories to do with psychoanalysis . . .':** Melanie Bayley, 'Alice's Adventures in Algebra: Wonderland Solved', *New Scientist*, 16 December 2009

CHAPTER ELEVEN: GOOD, SMART, COMMON SENSE

**'Twenty-one per cent had Higher Certificate':** Christopher Grey, *Decoding Organization: Bletchley Park, Codebreaking and Organization Studies*, 2012

ANSWERS

# CHAPTER ONE

## THE WORLD'S MOST FAMOUS CROSSWORD

*TELEGRAPH*

JANUARY 13TH 1942

| | | | | | | | | |
|---|---|---|---|---|---|---|---|---|
| ¹T | R | ²O | U | ³P | E | | ⁴S | ⁵H | ⁶O | ⁷R | ⁸T | C | U | T |
| I | | L | | S | | | O | | F | U | | A |
| ⁹P | R | I | V | E | T | | ¹⁰A | R | O | M | A | T | I | C |
| S | | V | | U | | ¹¹A | | D | | I | | T | | K |
| ¹²T | R | E | N | D | | ¹³G | R | ¹⁴E | A | T | D | E | A | L |
| A | | O | | ¹⁵O | W | E | | D | | | R | | | E |
| ¹⁶F | E | I | G | N | | ¹⁷N | E | ¹⁸W | A | ¹⁹R | K | | | |
| F | | L | | Y | | D | | R | | I | | ²⁰T | | ²¹S |
| | | ²²I | M | ²³P | A | L | E | | ²⁴G | U | I | S | E |
| ²⁵S | | ²⁶E | | I | | ²⁷A | S | H | | N | | N | | N |
| ²⁸C | E | N | ²⁹T | ³⁰R | E | B | I | T | | ³¹T | O | K | E | N |
| A | | A | O | | O | | H | | N | | L | | I |
| ³²L | A | M | E | D | O | G | S | | ³³R | A | C | I | N | G |
| E | | E | | I | | I | | | I | | N | | H |
| ³⁴S | I | L | E | N | C | E | R | | ³⁵A | L | I | G | H | T |

## 1

| 1 | 2 | 3 | 4 | 5 | 6 | 7 | 8 | | | | | | | |
|---|---|---|---|---|---|---|---|---|---|---|---|---|---|---|
| P | O | R | T | M | A | N | T | E | A | U | W | O | R | D |
| A | ■ | A | ■ | A | ■ | O | ■ | L | ■ | S | ■ | S | ■ | A |
| V | E | R | T | I | G | O | ■ | E | A | S | T | M | A | N |
| E | ■ | E | ■ | L | ■ | D | ■ | G | ■ | R | ■ | U | ■ | C |
| M | O | B | S | ■ | E | L | G | A | R | ■ | A | N | N | E |
| E | ■ | I | ■ | S | ■ | E | ■ | N | ■ | F | ■ | D | ■ | O |
| N | O | T | I | C | E | S | ■ | T | H | I | N | A | I | R |
| T | ■ | ■ | ■ | R | ■ | ■ | ■ | ■ | ■ | L | ■ | ■ | ■ | C |
| A | D | A | M | A | N | T | ■ | M | A | M | M | O | T | H |
| R | ■ | R | ■ | P | ■ | A | ■ | I | ■ | Y | ■ | N | ■ | E |
| T | A | M | E | ■ | B | U | R | N | S | ■ | M | E | S | S |
| I | ■ | E | ■ | O | ■ | N | ■ | U | ■ | F | ■ | S | ■ | T |
| S | U | N | S | P | O | T | ■ | T | R | A | C | T | O | R |
| T | ■ | I | ■ | U | ■ | O | ■ | E | ■ | I | ■ | E | ■ | A |
| S | T | A | R | S | A | N | D | S | T | R | I | P | E | S |

## 2

| 1 | 2 | 3 | 4 | 5 | 6 | 7 | 8 | | | | | | | |
|---|---|---|---|---|---|---|---|---|---|---|---|---|---|---|
| T | R | A | P | P | I | N | G | S | ■ | P | O | I | N | T |
| O | ■ | N | ■ | A | ■ | E | ■ | E | ■ | A | ■ | D | ■ | R |
| W | I | C | K | S | ■ | M | E | A | N | W | H | I | L | E |
| E | ■ | E | ■ | S | ■ | E | ■ | D | ■ | N | ■ | O | ■ | A |
| D | I | S | T | E | N | S | I | O | N | ■ | O | T | I | S |
| ■ | ■ | T | ■ | N | ■ | I | ■ | G | ■ | K | ■ | ■ | ■ | U |
| P | L | O | U | G | H | S | ■ | S | P | E | N | C | E | R |
| A | ■ | R | ■ | E | ■ | ■ | ■ | T | ■ | O | ■ | E | ■ | ■ |
| R | E | S | O | R | T | ■ | ■ | S | E | T | T | L | E | R |
| C | ■ | ■ | S | ■ | P | ■ | A | ■ | L | ■ | O | ■ | ■ | ■ |
| H | O | C | K | ■ | M | I | N | U | T | E | G | U | N | S |
| M | ■ | L | ■ | O | ■ | N | ■ | C | ■ | W | ■ | R | ■ | W |
| E | L | O | Q | U | E | N | C | E | ■ | E | M | I | L | E |
| N | ■ | U | ■ | T | ■ | E | ■ | R | ■ | L | ■ | N | ■ | E |
| T | O | D | A | Y | ■ | R | U | S | H | L | I | G | H | T |

## 3

```
S A V I N G   G R A C E
F   M   N   A   E   E   M   C
R O B E S   M A D E L E I N E
E   I   U   B   E   L   L   N
S A T U R N I N E   I S L E T
H   E   T   M   N   I   R
A C C E D E   S E M I T O N E
S   O   F   D   N   F
A l l F O U R S   P R E S T O
D   D   N   A G E   R
A M B L E   B A R L E Y M O W
I   A   M   J E L A A
S O T T O V O C E   E N T E R
Y   H   R   U C C E D
    N E W S L E T T E R S
```

## 4

```
  S A F E C O N D U C T
  B   N   Y   N   I   H   M
F R O G   E N C E P H A L I C
  E   E   S   E   P   R   E
O V E R A L L   B E A T I N G
  I   E   D R   R
S A T I S F I E D   L O O M S
  R   C   T   L   O   A
B Y R E S   L A D Y S M I T H
    L   C Y   S   E
S H E A T H E   M A N N E R S
  O   N   A R N O I
B R I D E S M A I D   B O A T
  N   E S G E L L
    T R U E H E A R T E D
```

## 5

| | | | | | | | | |
|---|---|---|---|---|---|---|---|---|
| ¹C | ²H | ³A | ⁴P | T | ⁵E | R | A | N | ⁶D | V | ⁷E | R | ⁸S | E |
| | O | | I | X | | I | | I | | R | | T | |
| ⁹F | L | Y | P | A | P | E | R | | ¹⁰G | O | S | H | E | N |
| | Y | | P | | E | | G | | I | | T | | E |
| ¹¹I | S | L | A | N | D | | ¹²U | N | T | O | W | A | R | D |
| | T | | | | I | | N | | | H | |
| ¹³C | O | ¹⁴W | H | E | E | L | | ¹⁵S | ¹⁶C | R | I | P | ¹⁷T | S |
| | N | | O | | N | | | A | | L | | W |
| ¹⁸H | E | R | M | I | T | S | | ¹⁹F | R | E | E | D | O | M |
| | | | E | | | ²⁰A | | P | | | | S |
| ²¹B | ²²N | A | T | U | ²³R | A | L | | ²⁴E | ²⁵M | B | L | E | M |
| | A | | | | R | E | M | | N | | O | | A |
| ²⁶C | O | B | U | R | G | | ²⁷O | U | T | C | A | S | T | S |
| | M | | T | | A | | S | | E | | S | | E |
| ²⁸L | I | G | H | T | L | I | T | E | R | A | T | U | R | E |

## 6

| | | | | | | | |
|---|---|---|---|---|---|---|---|
| | ¹B | E | ²A | C | O | ³N | ⁴S | F | ⁵I | E | ⁶L | D | ⁷ | |
| | | N | | H | | E | | E | | L | | A | | ⁸F |
| ⁹S | O | F | I | A | | ¹⁰A | R | C | | ¹¹S | A | L | M | I |
| I | | I | | S | | T | | U | | I | | A | | N |
| ¹²N | I | L | E | | ¹³C | H | A | N | G | E | L | I | N | G |
| G | | A | | ¹⁴U | | E | | D | | | | | | E |
| ¹⁵L | A | D | Y | B | I | R | ¹⁶D | | ¹⁷B | ¹⁸A | N | ¹⁹N | E | R |
| E | | E | | ²⁰D | I | ²¹G | | S | | E | | P |
| ²²M | O | S | L | E | M | | ²³P | A | S | S | O | V | E | R |
| I | | | | ²⁴S | | R | | U | | E | | I |
| ²⁵N | I | ²⁶G | H | ²⁷T | S | H | A | D | E | | ²⁸W | R | E | N |
| D | | O | | O | | A | | E | | ²⁹M | | M | | T |
| ³⁰E | L | B | O | W | | ³¹N | U | N | | ³²I | R | O | N | S |
| D | | B | | I | | K | | I | | N | | R |
| | ³³O | B | T | U | S | E | A | N | G | L | E | S |

## 7

| M | A | R | M | O | S | E | T | S |   | C |   | L |   | P |
|---|---|---|---|---|---|---|---|---|---|---|---|---|---|---|
|   | G | A |   | A | O |   | W | A | L | L | E | R |   | R |
| V | I | A | T | I | C | U | M |   | R |   | E |   | O |
|   | T |   | L |   | H |   | B | R | A | D | A | W | L | S |
| D | A | M | O | Z | E | L |   | O |   | G | E | E |   |
|   | T |   | C |   | T |   | P | A | R | A | L | L | E | L |
| M | O | C | K | S |   |   |   | C |   | M |   | L |   | Y |
| A |   | H |   | A | N | T |   | H | U | E |   | Y |   | T |
| T |   | I |   | C |   | I |   |   | S | I | N | C | E |   |
| R | A | C | K | R | E | N | T |   | M |   | M |   | O |   |
| I |   | A |   | I |   | G |   | R | A | S | P | I | N | G |
| C | A | N | I | S | T | E | R |   | N |   | R |   | V |   |
| I |   | E |   | T |   |   | E | N | T | R | E | P | O | T |
| D | U | R | B | A | N |   | L |   | U |   | S |   | K |   |
| E |   | Y |   | N |   | D | Y | N | A | S | T | I | E | S |

## 8

| C | H | E | E | K | B | Y | J | O | W | L |   | P | O | M |
|---|---|---|---|---|---|---|---|---|---|---|---|---|---|---|
| A |   | M |   | O |   | E |   | R |   | O |   | A |   | I |
| R | U | M | O | U | R | S |   | D | U | C | K | I | N | G |
| D |   | A |   | M |   | T |   | E |   | A |   | N |   | N |
|   |   | M | I | R | R | O | R |   | R | A | T | I | O |   |
| E |   | F |   | S |   | E |   |   | A |   | B |   | N |   |
| S | P | I | N | S | T | E | R |   | C | O | W | R | I | E |
| C |   | N |   |   | N |   | B |   |   | U |   | T |   |   |
| A | K | I | M | B | O |   | M | A | R | M | O | S | E | T |
| L |   | S |   | A |   | T |   | N |   | I |   | H |   | E |
| A | C | T | O | N |   | I | N | D | I | C | T |   |   |   |
| T |   | E |   | A |   | V |   | I |   | H |   | S |   | U |
| O | T | R | A | N | T | O |   | T | R | A | I | L | E | R |
| R |   | R |   | A |   | L |   | T |   | E |   | A |   | A |
| S | E | E |   | S | P | I | R | I | T | L | E | V | E | L |

215

## 9

```
B O G U S   P A G E A N T R Y
O   A   A   H     V   U   O
W H I S K E R S   K I T T E N
W   T   E   E   M   D   E   G
I B E X   A N N U L   B L U E
N   R   C   O   D   T   A
D     B A L L A D M O N G E R   R
O   E   B   O   L   I   E   E
W E D D I N G B E L L S   C
    E   N   I   H   S   C   L
F A N E   O S I E R   B A B A
R   T   N   T   A   H   N   I
A R A B I N   A D D E N D U M
N   T   S   E   R   I   E
C H E R I S H E D   B I D E D
```

## 10

```
D E S C A N T   A N N A B E L
U   P   U   R     O   L   I
F R A C T I O U S   R H O M B
    N   U   Y   T   S   N   E
B I G A M Y   L A V E N D E R
O   L   N   A   N   M   E   T
T O E B   B L I N D A L L E Y
T     F   A   A   N       H
L A C K L U S T R E   R I T A
E   A   O   T   Y   M   N   L
P A L A T I A L   T A S S E L
A   A   I   I   L   N   T
R E B E L   R O A S T B E E F
T   A   L   M   L   A   E
Y A R D A R M   B L E N D E R
```

# CHAPTER TWO

## THE MORSE MASTERMINDS

### 1

### THE FIRST MORSE MESSAGE

OUGHT TO DO GOOD THROUGHOUT THAT WAR.

### 2

### DISASTER TRANSMISSION

JANUARY 1945. BOAT SANK. RESCUE OPERATION IN PROGRESS.

### 3

### KEYBOARD CRISIS

**a)** IMMINENT DEPARTURE. BE PREPARED TO QUIT SAFE HOUSE WITHOUT DELAY.

**b)** PENELOPE ARRIVES PORTSMOUTH 4PM!

# 4

## OVER TO YOU

•— •—• •—• ——— —— •— —• —•—• •••• • •••/
••— —• —•• • •—•/ ••—• •• •—• •./ •—• • •• —•
••—• ——— •—• —•—• • —••/ •— •• •—•/ •—• • —•—•
—•—• •./ •——— ••— —• • —••••/ —• ——— •—• ——
•— —• —•• —•—— .

# 5

## HEARTBEAT

**a)** The square root of 25 is 5, which is V in Roman numerals. V in Morse code has the beats •••—, which is the opening rhythm of Beethoven's Fifth Symphony.

In 1940, the BBC began transmitting to Europe with the 'V' (for Victory) signal in Morse code, and continued with this until 1945 and beyond.

**b)** The vowels U and O in Morse beat out ••— ———, the opening line of the song 'Happy Birthday to You'.

**c)** 9T in Morse beats out ————• —, the first line of 'God Save the King'. Everyone please stand.

## 6

### MORALE BOOSTER

TO COMMANDER IN CHIEF AFLOAT, I THANK YOU IN THE NAME
OF THE ENTIRE GERMAN PEOPLE. ADOLF HITLER.

## 7

### DASH IT ALL, DOT!

**a)** This word uses letters in Morse code signal made up of one dot or dash.
**b)** This word uses letters made up of two dots and/or dashes.
**c)** This word uses letters made up of three dots and/or dashes.
**d)** This word uses letters made up of four dots and/or dashes.
**e)** And finally, SHE is made up of letters made only of dots and the letters in TOM are composed solely of dashes.

## 8

### UNDER PRESSURE

```
•• — • • — • ––– — — / •• — • –––– • –––– ––––– ••• — — /
• •• ••• • • — •• • / — ––– / — • — • • — • —— • — • — ••
— • / •• — — ••• ––– • — — / — ••• • — • —— • — •• — • — • .
/ — •• — — ••• • / — • •• — — — — ••• • • — • / •••• — • /
• — •• • • — — • — •• •• — • —— • / •• — • • — • ––– –––
— •• •• — • —— • / • — — • — •• / — •• • — • • — •• — • ••
— • —— • . /
```

# 9

## BLITZ

**a)** JAPAN/ITALY

**b)** MALTA/RHINE

**c)** PARIS/DOVER

**d)** LONDON/WARSAW

**e)** BERLIN/MOSCOW

# 10

## SWITCHBOARD

YONDER/RECTOR (TRANSFER TO SQUARE 1) RETORT/TARIFF/ FINISH/HALVES/SYSTEM (TRANSFER TO SQUARE 2) MOSAIC/ CIRCUS/SQUEAK/KNIGHT/TURRET (TRANSFER TO SQUARE 3) TORRID/DIRECT/TEAPOT (TRANSFER TO SQUARE 4) TEMPLE/ ENDING/GALLOP (TRANSFER TO SQUARE 5) POTION/NORMAL/ LINTEL/LIQUID/DYNAMO (TRANSFER TO SQUARE 6) OPTION/ NEBULA/ARMADA.

| N | E | B | U | L | A | R | M | A | D | A |
|---|---|---|---|---|---|---|---|---|---|---|
| O | I | T | P | O | L | L | A | G | N | I |
| S | Y | S | T | E | M | P | L | E | N | D |
| E | V | L | A | H | S | I | N | I | F | F |
| U | R | R | E | T | O | R | T | A | R | I |
| T | H | G | I | N | K | A | E | U | Q | S |
| A | M | O | S | A | I | C | I | R | C | U |
| N | Y | D | I | U | Q | I | L | E | T | N |
| O | T | I | O | N | O | R | M | A | L | I |
| P | A | E | T | C | E | R | I | D | I | R |
| Y | O | N | D | E | R | E | C | T | O | R |

220

# CHAPTER THREE

## THE ENIGMA CONNECTIONS

## 1

### X MACHINE

| | | | |
|---|---|---|---|
| 1 = X | | 14 = O |
| 2 = F | | 15 = R |
| 3 = H | | 16 = G |
| 4 = N | | 17 = I |
| 5 = P | | 18 = J |
| 6 = B | | 19 = S |
| 7 = L | | 20 = W |
| 8 = Y | | 21 = M |
| 9 = A | | 22 = U |
| 10 = C | | 23 = V |
| 11 = D | | 24 = T |
| 12 = E | | 25 = Q |
| 13 = K | | 26 = Z |

# 2

## RATION BOOK

Item a) rationed in September 1939 was PETROL. The other items are:

**b)** BACON
**c)** BUTTER
**d)** SUGAR
**e)** CHEESE
**f)** EGGS
**g)** MEAT
**h)** MARGARINE

# 3

## CAPITAL CODE

The message reads: MEET IN HUT EIGHT AT SIX. The numbers refer to how many straight lines make up a capital letter. The list is as follows:

0 – C O S U
1 – B D G I J P Q
2 – L R T V X
3 – A F H K N Y Z
4 – E M W

From the permutations on offer, the given answer can be formed. Hut Eight was famously associated with one of Bletchley's most prestigious names, Alan Turing.

# 4

## CONNECTIONS

The message reads: GO TO RED HOUSE BY BOAT AND ON FOOT.
The pairings are:

CART (ON) WARD

COLTS (FOOT) PRINT

ERR (AND) IRON

GREEN (HOUSE) KEEPER

GRUB (BY) GONE

HAT (RED) RAW

HITHER (TO) NIGHT

LIFE (BOAT) SWAIN

UNDER (GO) SLING

# 5

## SET SQUARE

The cipher uses a 5 x 5 square with alphabetical letters written in rows across. As said in the clues, X and Y share the same square. Both the rows and the columns are also numbered 1 to 5. Every letter has a two-number reference. Take the number of the row first, then the number of the column in which the letter appears, e.g. H appears in row 2 and column 3, so it is written as 23. 'It's all Greek to me' is an idiom that is quite correct in this case. The system is credited to Polybius, who lived in the second century BC.

**a)** COME, FRIENDLY BOMBS, AND FALL ON SLOUGH
(Written by John Betjeman in the inter-war years.)

**b)** LAST NIGHT, I DREAMT I WENT TO MANDERLEY AGAIN
(Daphne du Maurier's opening to the novel Rebecca. )

**c)** DON'T PUT YOUR DAUGHTER ON THE STAGE, MRS WORTHINGTON (A line from Noel Coward's song.)

# 6

## CARD CONUNDRUM

The message is: SOON BE TEA TIME.

The keys are the card numbers and the names of the suits. The first word SOON is made from the fifth letter in CLUBS, the fifth letter in DIAMONDS (twice), and the sixth letter in DIAMONDS. BE is made from the fourth letter in CLUBS and the fifth letter in SPADES. TEA is letters 5, 2 and 3 from the word HEARTS. TIME is the fifth letter of HEARTS, the second of DIAMONDS, the fourth of DIAMONDS and the fifth of SPADES.

# 7

## CODE WHEEL

The code number is 26. To find the number in the centre take a quarter of the circle at a time. The numbers in the bottom left quarter, when added, produce a total of 30 in the outer ring and 22 in the middle ring. Take 22 from 30 to leave 8. Add this to the third ring and the total is 22. With the top left quarter the outer total (22) is 8 less than the total of the next ring (14), and if you add 8 to the total of the inner ring (10) you get 18. In the top right quarter the outer segment totals 18, which is 8 less than the total of the next ring (10), so if you add 8 to the 26 from the inner ring, the total is 34.

In the final quarter, therefore, the outer ring totals 14, the next ring totals 10. So 14 − 10 = 4, which is added to the inner ring (22) to give you 26 – the final mystery number.

# 8

## DICING WITH DANGER

In each row the first number tallies with the number of spots that are in the centre of the dice, across all five of them. The second number is the total of spots that surround these centre spots. And you can find the third number by adding up the spots that remain. So the final row reads: 366. The second and penultimate years of the Second World War, 1940 and 1944, were both leap years and therefore had 366 days.

# 9

## THE UNKNOWN QUANTITY

The ? stands for number 6, which represents a letter A. The words formed are:

**a)** EGG

**b)** GENIE

**c)** IMAGINE

**d)** ENGINE

**e)** MEANING

**f)** INANE

**g)** MANGE

**h)** ENIGMA

# 10

## JIGSAW CODE

The message reads:

CAPTAIN TONIGHT RADIO OFFICER.

| C | H | E | A | T |   | T | A | P |   | C | A | C | H | E |
|---|---|---|---|---|---|---|---|---|---|---|---|---|---|---|
| O |   | M |   | R | O |   | E |   | U |   | H |   |   | T |
| C | A | P | T | A | I | N |   | R | E | F | R | E | S | H |
| O |   | E |   | M |   | I |   | F |   | F |   | R |   | E |
| A | C | R | E |   | A | G | R | E | E |   | P | I | E | R |
|   |   | O |   | A |   | H |   | C |   | R |   | S |   |   |
| A | C | R | O | B | A | T |   | T | E | A | C | H | E | R |
| R |   |   | Y |   |   |   |   | D |   |   |   |   |   | Y |
| C | L | A | S | S | I | C |   | E | P | I | S | O | D | E |
|   | C |   | S |   | R |   | X |   | O |   | F |   |   |   |
| E | C | H | O |   | V | O | C | A | L |   | A | F | A | R |
| X |   | I |   | I |   | C |   | M |   | K |   | I |   | E |
| C | H | E | E | T | A | H |   | P | A | N | A | C | H | E |
| E |   | V |   | C |   | E |   | L |   | O |   | E |   | D |
| L | E | E | C | H |   | T | I | E |   | T | U | R | N | S |

# CHAPTER FOUR

## MIND YOUR SECRET LANGUAGE

## 1

### THE LANGUAGE OF KAT

#### GRAMMATICAL RULES OF KAT:

Nouns: end in –eg or –egg if they are plural
Verbs: end in –k in present tense; end in –kel in present continuous
Word order: there is no set order

#### GLOSSARY:

casal: home
da: from
fee: four
fel: watch
fu: away
grih (sing.)/grihegg (pl.):
    mouse/mice
jonelegg: children
ke: two
kit (sing.)/kitegg (pl.): cat(s)
mangak: eat

mu: three
persek: chase
piacak: like
pun: meat
ro: on
tolg (sing.)/toleeg (pl.): dog(s)
uchak/ucha: walk/the walk
und: and
vink: steal
wolg (sing.)/woleeg (pl.): lady/
    ladies

ANSWERS:

N.B. Because there is no set word order, there can be variations within these answers. So for example in 1 b) the answer could also be 'the mice are watching the ladies'.

1.  **a)**  The cats and dogs walk home.
    **b)**  The ladies are watching the mice.

2.  **a)**  kitegg und toleeg piacak wolg
    **b)**  toleeg persekel kitegg casal

3.  **a)**  Three dogs chase two ladies home.
    **b)**  The mouse watches the two cats.

4.  **a)**  tolg fel kit und kit fel grih
    **b)**  tolg und kit fel jonelegg uchak casal

5.  **a)**  The three ladies and the children eat the meat.
    **b)**  The dog eats meat on the walk home.

6.  **a)**  wolg fel tolg vink pun
    **b)**  ke kitegg persek grih fu da casal

# 2

*FINNEGANS WAKE*

Interpretations below:

'**riverrun**' The river running, some presume past the Garden of Eden.

'**Past Eve and Adam's**' Further evidence of the Garden of Eden. But recently Garratt Barden, a subscriber to the New York Review of Books, pointed out that Eve and Adam's was also a nickname given to a church in Dublin that stood at a quay on the River Liffey.

'**Commodious vicus of recirculation**' Here, with this puzzling cryptic crossword phrase, the interpretations multiply dazzlingly; 'Commodious Vicus' has the sound of a Roman emperor – like Commodus? Yet it also suggests 'commode', which James Joyce frequently used for comic effect. Vicus of recirculation? Here, there are some who have spotted a sideways reference to the renaissance historian Giambattista Vico. Fitting in with 'recirculation', Vico championed the idea of cycles in history. Alternatively, there was a Vico Road in Dublin, from which one could see . . .

'**Howth Castle**' A favoured James Joyce landmark. This brings us back to Dublin Bay, where the castle stands. It has been noted that Dublin Bay bends and swerves as it comes around to Howth.

**Sir Tristram** Many of the figures in the book are split into two; and Sir Tristram can either be Sir Armory Tristram, the fifteenth century figure who had Howth Castle built; or Tristram who fell in love with the beautiful Iseult (becoming Tristan and Isolde).

**Violer d'amores** Again, the interpretations split: a violer might be one who plays the viola, in which case here is romance; or equally, this might suggest violation, and the phrase imply rape.

**Passencore** Or perhaps – in the style of Mavis Lever – we might see this from a different angle as 'pas encore', the French phrase meaning 'not yet'.

**His penisolate war** A dizzying range of suggestions: a reference to the Peninsular War from Napoleonic times; a compound word made from 'pen' and 'isolate' suggesting both Joyce's artistic outsiderness but also – once again – Giambattista Vico, who took up his pen alone to write his philosophy of history.

**Topsawyer's rocks** A landmark in Dublin, Georgia, USA, on the Oconee river. Also: 'Mr Topsawyer' is a figure invented by a lying waiter in Dicken's David Copperfield, refusing to give young David the full pint of stout he paid for on the grounds that 'Mr Topsawyer' had drunk a full pint and dropped down dead.

**Mishe mishe to tauftauf** Mishe Mishe are the first words of a Jewish holiday song; added to this, the phrase sounds like one radio operator addressing another by code names.

**Thuart Peatrick** 'Thuart' has been read as either 'thwart' or 'thou art'; 'Peatrick' a blending of the saints Peter and Patrick.

**Kidscad buttended a bland old isaac** The compound word 'kidscad' is thought by some to be slang for a violent gang; 'buttended' similarly is slang for being struck with a gun; Isaac is the blind Biblical figure. The sleeper who is dreaming this text feels under attack.

**Vanessy** This is taken to be a part reference to 18th century writer Jonathan Swift and his association with Esther Vanhomrigh, out of whose name – the 'Van' and affectionate diminutive 'Essa' – he originated the name 'Vanessa'.

**Sosie Sesthers** Sosie is French for twin or doppelganger; sesthers a mix of 'sisters' and 'Esther' (see 'Vanessy'); sosie also suggests 'saucy'; yet these sisters are part of a troubling and transgressive father/daughter element in the pages to come.

**Twone Nathandjoe** The first word might be a concertina'd 'two-in-to-one', a consistent leitmotif in the Wake. We might again be dealing with doubles 'Nathan' and 'Joe'. Or 'Nathandjoe' might be a flipped compound of Jonathan. 'Nath', it has been pointed out, was also a High King of Ireland some 1,500 years ago.

**Jhem or Shen** Possibly yet more twins (Shen being the son of another character who will appear later). 'Shem' with an M was one of Noah's sons; and 'Shem' is Hebrew for 'name' in the sense of 'renown'. Conversely, when read aloud, 'Jhem or Shen' sounds a little like a drunk pronouncing the name of his favourite Irish whiskey (and a brand very popular in Joyce's day) – Jamiesons.

**Regginbrow** A compound of German and English, resulting in another term for 'rainbow'.

**bababadalgharaghtakamminarronnkonnbronntonnerronntuonn-thunntrovarrhounawnskawntoohoohoordenenthernuk!** Over this, there seems some agreement: this is the sound of a mighty thunder crack – a crack of doom – the crack that signifies man's fall.

**Pftjschute** Descriptive of the sleeper's fall, possibly combining the French expression of disdain, 'pft', with 'chute'.

**Tumptytumtoes** Contriving to weave Humpty Dumpty (another faller) together with the sense of a melodic humming to oneself.

**Since devlinsfirst loved livvy** Again, the potential intepretations multiply dizzyingly; returning to themes of Eden, and of a world of mythological giants, 'since' might be 'sins', 'devlins' devils, and 'livvy' the term for the daughters of man. Alternatively, Albert Devlin was a Dublin politician of some significance; 'Devlin' might be the sleeper mangling 'Dublin'; and 'livvy' might be a reworking of the River Liffey.

# CHAPTER FIVE

## THE CHESSBOARD WAR

### 1

#### OPENING GAMBIT

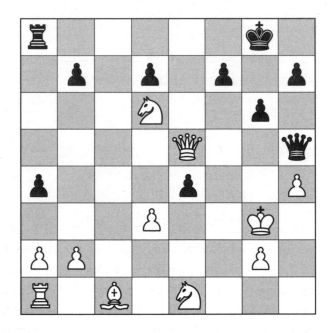

# 2

## EXCHANGES

The word that won't fit is ROOKS, which is the answer to the clue 'Crows'.

| Exchange 1 | Exchange 2 | Exchange 3 |
|------------|------------|------------|
| W H I T E  | C H E S S  | M O V E D  |
| W H I N E  | C R E S S  | M O V E S  |
| C H I N E  | C R A S S  | D O V E S  |
| C H I N K  | B R A S S  | D O T E S  |
| C H I C K  | B R A T S  | D A T E S  |
| C L I C K  | B O A T S  | D A R E S  |
| C L A C K  | B O A R S  | D A R N S  |
|            |            | D A W N S  |
| B L A C K  | B O A R D  |            |
|            |            | P A W N S  |

# 3

## MIDDLE GAME – KING'S GAMBIT

The informer is called EDWARD GEORGE JAMES. The positions of the named pieces provide the clue. All are in the column, or file, of the white king. The knight is in the square that in notation is K8. (The letter K comes from KING. The clue is in the title of the puzzle.) The bishop is in K6 and the queen is in K2. The references link to names of kings of England. There have been EIGHT kings named Henry and Edward. There have been SIX kings named George, and TWO kings named Charles and James. The number of letters in the chesspiece names written above the board indicate how many letters there are in the hidden names, which you can write in the empty spaces below the words. The six letters of KNIGHT means Henry can be discounted and Edward is the first name, as it is also

233

six letters long so fits the space available. For BISHOP, George is the only option, and the name matches the number of letters. The five letters in QUEEN means Charles can be discounted and James written in place in the five spaces.

# 4

## KNIGHT MOVES

FREEDOM IS IN PERIL DEFEND IT WITH ALL YOUR MIGHT. These words featured on a government poster of the late 1930s when war was looming.

| A | ♞ | Z | ²R | ⁷M | ¹²P | ¹⁷D | C |
|---|---|---|---|---|---|---|---|
| B | ³E | ⁶O | ¹³E | ¹⁶L | ¹⁹F | ⁸I | ¹¹N |
| ⁵D | ¹⁴R | ¹F | ²⁰E | ³¹L | ¹⁰I | Z | ¹⁸E |
| ³⁸G | X | ⁴E | ¹⁵I | J | ²¹N | ³⁰L | ⁹S |
| Q | U | ³⁹H | ³²Y | ²⁹A | ³⁴U | X | ²²D |
| U | ³⁷I | Y | ³⁵R | P | ²³I | ²⁶I | O |
| K | ⁴⁰I | L | Z | ³³O | ²⁸H | G | ²⁴T |
| L | P | ³⁶M | D | N | ²⁵W | N | ²⁷T |

# 5

## ENDGAME

| WORDS USED IN CHESS | LINK WORD | ENDGAME |
|---|---|---|
| WHITE | CHRISTMAS | CARD |
| KINGS | CROSS | ROADS |
| SQUARE | DANCE | HALL |
| BISHOPS | GATE | POST |
| KNIGHT | HOOD | WINK |
| BLACK | MAGIC | CIRCLE |
| PIECE | MEAL | TICKET |
| CHECK | POINT | DUTY |
| PAWN | SHOP | KEEPER |
| QUEEN | VICTORIA | PLUM |

# CHAPTER SIX

## THE CODES FROM THE MUMMY'S TOMB

### 1

### SIGN HERE

Using the four given elements, this combination is the only one not pictured.

Left to right: 𓀀 𓊽 𓆣 𓁐

### 2

### THE FIRST DIG

The clue is in the wall itself. The wall follows a series of turns. The first corner turns to the right. The second to the left. The third corner turns to the left. This pattern is repeated and followed throughout.

The only exception is the section of wall in the middle right of the plan, where the tunnel narrows between the walls. The turn should go left, instead it goes right. Beyond that wall will lie the secret burial chamber.

### 3

### ON REFLECTION

Pattern number 4.

# 4

## RESEARCH NOTES

**a)** All the words are formed from the letters in the word PYRAMID.

**b)** The central two letters from each word, taken in left to right order, spell out ROSETTA STONE.

**c)** Each word is an anagram. Together they read: ACT NOW AND SOLVE ENIGMAS!

# 5

## RESTORATION

Pattern number 3.

# 6

## PYRAMID BUILDING

The words fit back as follows:

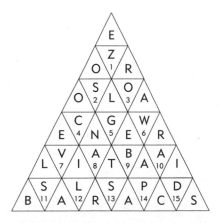

The code word is: SCARAB. This can be found reading backwards on the bottom row of the pyramid, in the triangles without a number.

# 7

## EYE OF HORUS

# 8

## HIDDEN MEANINGS

Words are concealed by linking a word ending with the start of another word, revealing the following:

**a)** CODE

**b)** TOMB

**c)** DYNASTY

**d)** CATACOMB

**e)** EYE

**f)** MEANING

# 9

## MUMMY'S MENU

**a)** SOUP

**b)** HAM

**c)** PIE

**d)** MASH

**e)** PEAS

**f)** APPLES

**g)** PEARS

**h)** PLUMS

# 10

## THREE-SIDED

**a)** The number in the pyramid is 18. The outer numbers are multiplied together and then the total is divided by ten to produce the number inside the pyramid.

**b)** Each triangle represents three months of the year in reverse order, starting from December. The letter sequence is the initials of the first and last of these three months, with the corresponding days in each month round the outside (so the first triangle has D and O for December and October, with the numbers 31, 30 and 31 round the outside). For the final triangle, the letters inside are MJ (for March and January) and the numbers are 31 on the left, 28 on the right, and 31 below the pyramid (29 instead of 28 for February is acceptable, but only in leap year!).

**c)** The symbol inside is 12ΩΣ. The mystic symbols are just numerals with a mirror image opposite. Add up the numbers to produce the number inside the pyramid. So 3, 4 and 5 are the outer numbers.

# CHAPTER SEVEN

## MUSIC, MAESTROS!

### 1

### MAJOR TO MINOR

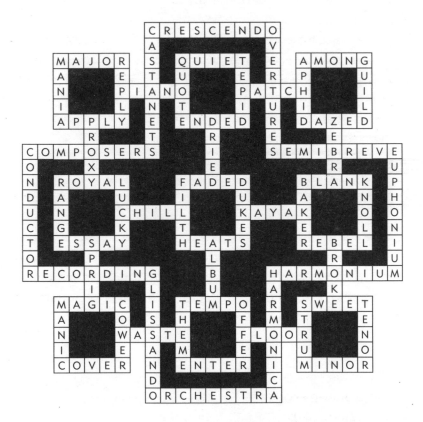

# 2

## COMPOSITION STUDY

Michael also plays the ukulele. In each case the initial letters of the instruments played can be arranged to form the name of a famous composer. All initial letters are involved and they can be used more than once if needed. David plays the recorder, accordion, mandolin, oboe, trumpet and zither, making MOZART. Jean plays the recorder, accordion, saxophone, ukulele and tuba, making STRAUSS (letter S used more than once). Susan plays the recorder, accordion, euphonium, guitar and lute, making ELGAR. Michael plays the recorder, clarinet and piano plus three of the instruments Susan plays. We are told he does not play the accordion. Therefore, he plays two instruments from the euphonium, guitar and lute. Initial letter combinations must be R, C, P + either E, G / E, L / or G, L. The addition of an extra instrument with a U for ukulele gives the combination recorder, clarinet, piano, euphonium, lute and ukulele from which PURCELL can be made.

# 3

## PICTUREDROME

The question mark is replaced by a letter U. The name of the puzzle is a clue pointing to films. All the groups of letters can be rearranged to make the names of famous musical films that were extremely popular in the 1940s (and still are today). The numbers indicate the number of words in the title of each:

**1.** FANTASIA
**2.** TOP HAT
**3.** ROAD TO SINGAPORE
**4.** THE WIZARD OF OZ
**5.** MEET ME IN ST LOUIS

# 4

## PRELUDE

The notes to the solo horn player reads: CHANGE EACH CODE BEFORE DANGER. Letters from the word HORN are already in place, leaving spaces to be filled. The missing letters come from the piece of music. In standard music notation, every note is named with a letter from A to G. (Reading upwards, the letters in the four spaces between horizontal lines are F, A, C and E, and the letters straddling the five horizontal lines are E, G, B, D and F. Notes appearing above and below the printed lines follow the same established pattern.) The time-signature numbers, appearing on the left of the first bar, give the key to selecting letters, so 3 over 4 points to the THIRD note in each bar (each new bar is indicated by a vertical line across the staves). The corresponding letter is transferred to the message.

# 5

## QUINTET

The question marks are replaced by the letters W and U (representing the letters R and P in code). There are five different musical instruments featured in the quintet. They are all found by moving backwards in the alphabet from the starting letters. In group 1, move one letter backwards, so that the starter G becomes F, and so on. In group 2, move two letters backwards, so that the starter letter R becomes a P. Group 3 moves three letters backwards, group 4 moves four letters backwards, and group 5 moves five letters backwards.

1. FLUTE
2. PIANO
3. TUBA
4. TRUMPET
5. HARP

# 6

## ENSEMBLE

JENNY / GUITAR / SCHUBERT / FOURTH
MALCOLM / FLUTE / BEETHOVEN / FIRST
NEVILLE / OBOE / GERSHWIN / FIFTH
PHYLLIS / PIANO / HANDEL / SECOND
SHEILA / CLARINET / KERN / THIRD

# 7

## COUNTERPOINT

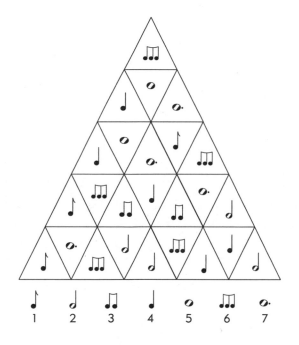

# 8

## RECITATIVE

The song is dedicated to the orchestra, as the entire lyrics are formed using the letters in the word ORCHESTRA.

# 9

## NINTH SYMPHONY

| # | ⌣ | 𝄆 | 𝄢 | ♮ | ♭ | – | 𝄞 | > |
|---|---|---|---|---|---|---|---|---|
| – | > | ♭ | ⌣ | 𝄆 | 𝄞 | # | 𝄢 | ♮ |
| ♮ | 𝄞 | 𝄢 | # | – | > | 𝄆 | ♭ | ⌣ |
| ⌣ | ♮ | # | 𝄞 | > | – | ♭ | 𝄆 | 𝄢 |
| 𝄆 | ♭ | – | ♮ | # | 𝄢 | > | ⌣ | 𝄞 |
| 𝄞 | 𝄢 | > | 𝄆 | ♭ | ⌣ | ♮ | – | # |
| > | 𝄆 | ⌣ | – | 𝄢 | ♮ | 𝄞 | # | ♭ |
| 𝄢 | – | ♮ | ♭ | 𝄞 | # | ⌣ | > | 𝄆 |
| ♭ | # | 𝄞 | > | ⌣ | 𝄆 | 𝄢 | ♮ | – |

244

# 10

## SERENADE

**a)** EVIL. The seven given words of four letters can make two word squares that read the same across and down, with one word missing from the first square. The missing word reads E ? I L. EVIL is the only option.

| V | E | R | A |
|---|---|---|---|
| E | V | I | L |
| R | I | F | T |
| A | L | T | O |

| O | P | A | L |
|---|---|---|---|
| P | O | N | Y |
| A | N | O | N |
| L | Y | N | N |

**b)** GRACIE FIELDS is the singer. Start by arranging the given words downwards in columns. In the third and final rows, the singer's name is revealed.

| E | B | C | R | U | C |
|---|---|---|---|---|---|
| N | O | H | E | N | H |
| G | R | A | C | I | E |
| U | Z | S | A | T | A |
| L | O | T | L | E | T |
| F | I | E | L | D | S |

# CHAPTER EIGHT

## HIGHLAND REELS AND CROQUET LAWNS

### 1

### HEAD OVER REELS

**a)**  **b)**

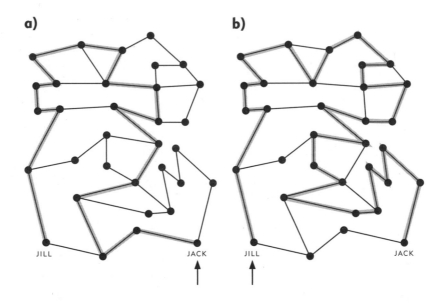

**a)** Jack to Jill 18 moves.

**b)** Jill to Jack 29 moves.

## 2

### TAKE YOUR PARTNERS

BLACKMAIL, CARAPACE, COVERAGE, CUPBOARD, INTERVIEW,
KEYHOLE, PARTRIDGE, PLAINTIFF, SEASON

## 3

### THE DEVIOUS DEVISER

There are 32 triangles.

## 4

### STEP TO A REEL

**a)** *Three-couple reel*
Sal has chosen couples whose names can be made from a single row of letters from a qwerty typewriter. The names Prue and Peter come from the top row of letters. The names Terri and Roy also come from the top row. The names Ada and Alf come from the middle row of letters. Sal's name can be formed from the middle row of letters of a qwerty typewriter as well.

**b)** *Five-couple reel*
AVA, MAX, TAMMY and TOMMY are on the dance floor and their names are made from capital letters that are symmetrical. The three couples who join them must be similarly named. The six lucky dancers are therefore: AMY, MATT, MAY, OTTO, TIM and VIV.

# 5

## GET IN LINE

| | | | | |
|---|---|---|---|---|
| ■ | * | ■ | ○ | ○ |
| * | ■ | ■ | ○ | * |
| ○ | ○ | * | ■ | ■ |
| ○ | * | ○ | ○ | ○ |
| ■ | ○ | * | * | ○ |

# 6

## BLETCHLEY RING

Judith, Thomas, Astrid, Dougal, Alice, Cecil, Lionel, Nellie, Eleanor, Norman, Angela, Elaine, Neville, Leah, Herbert, Bertram, Amy, Myra, Ralph, Phyllis, Sid, Dick.

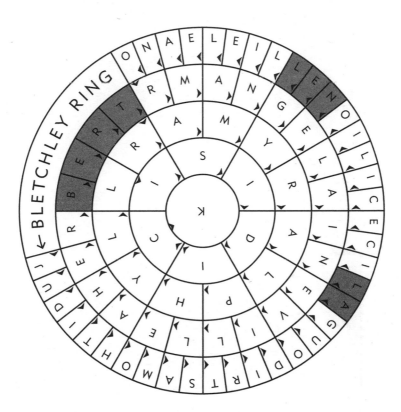

# 7

## FOUR TIME

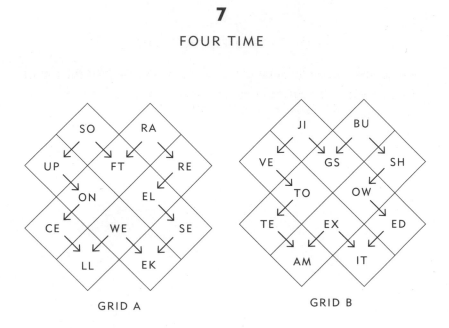

GRID A                    GRID B

Grid A: Else, Seek, Week, Well, Cell, Once, Upon, Soup, Soft, Raft, Rare, Reel.

Grid B: Owed, Edit, Exit, Exam, Team, Tote, Veto, Jive, Jigs, Bugs, Bush, Show.

# 8

## AROUND THE FLOOR

It will take eleven moves, 6 for the gentleman and 5 for the lady, before they meet up again in Corner E.

# 9

## DIAMOND FORMATION

The question mark is replaced by a 4. Start with the 1 at the top of the diamond. Add one to make 2.

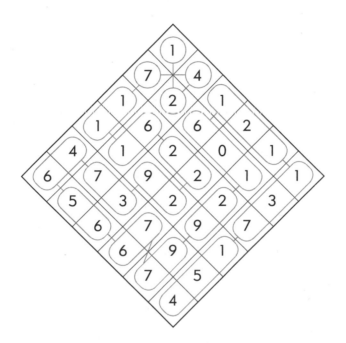

Then add two to make 4. Then add three to make 7, and so on. You will end up with the following sequence: 1, 2, 4, 7, 11, 16, 22, 29, 37, 46, 56, 67, 79, 92, 106, 121, 137. You can trace this sequence of numbers through the grid, each separate digit in its own square. The final number is the seventeenth move, so that is added to 137, giving the final number of 154.

# 10

## CROQUET CHALLENGE

Multiply the hoop values by the number of times a score has been registered (e.g. hoop value 20 x 3 = 60). Add the numbers together to make the total points scored between all the players, which is 213. If you divide this total score between the three players, you discover each finished with 71 points. From the information provided, the three combinations of hoops that can achieve this score in six goes are:

**a)**  1 + 2 + 3 + 5 + 10 + 50 = 71.

**b)**  1 + 2 + 3 + 20 + 20 + 25 = 71.

**c)**  1 + 5 + 10 + 10 + 20 + 25 = 71.

Roger scored 25 in three attempts. 2 + 3 + 20 is the only combination on offer. Therefore Roger's scorecard is line B. Sandra scored a 2, which means she could not have scorecard C, where the number does not appear. Thomas must have scorecard C. Sandra is left with scorecard A including the maximum 50.

# CHAPTER NINE

## IT ALL ADDS UP

## 1

### MRS TIMPKINS'S AGE

The age of the younger at marriage is always the same as the number of years that expire before the elder becomes twice her age, if he was three times as old at marriage. In our case it was eighteen years afterwards ; therefore Mrs Timpkins was eighteen years of age on the wedding-day, and her husband fifty-four.

## 2

### A TIME PUZZLE

Twenty-six minutes

## 3

### DIGITS AND SQUARES

The top row must be one of the four following numbers : 192, 219, 273, 327. The first was the example given.

# 4

## THE FOUR SEVENS

The way to write four sevens with simple arithmetical signs so that they represent 100 is as follows:

$$\frac{7}{.7} \times \frac{7}{.7} = 100$$

Of course the fraction 7 over decimal 7 (0.7) is the same as 70 divided by 7, or 10. Then 10 multiplied by 10 is 100, and there you are! It will be seen that this solution applies equally to any number that you may substitute for 7.

# 5

## VISITING THE TOWNS

Note that there are six towns from which only two roads issue. Thus 1 must lie between 9 and 12 in the circular route. Mark these two roads as settled. Similarly, mark 9, 5, 14, and 4, 8, 14, and 10, 6, 15, and 10, 2, 13, and 3, 7, 13. All these roads must be taken. Then you will find that he must go from 4 to 15, as 13 is closed, and that he is compelled to take 3, 11, 16, and also 16, 12. Thus, there is only one route, as follows: 1, 9, 5, 14, 8, 4, 15, 6, 10, 2, 13, 7, 3, 11, 16, 12, 1, or its reverse – reading the line the other way. Seven roads are not used.

# 6

## NEXT-DOOR NEIGHBOURS

Mr Jupp 39, Mrs Jupp 34, Julia 14, and Joe 13; Mr Simkin 42, Mrs Simkin 40, Sophy 10, and Sammy 8.

# 7

## CURIOUS NUMBERS

The three smallest numbers, in addition to 48, are 1,680, 57,120, and 1,940,448. It will be found that 1,681 and 841, 57,121 and 28,561, 1,940,449 and 970,225, are respectively the squares of 41 and 29,239 and 169, 1,393 and 985.

# 8

## THE FARMER AND HIS SHEEP

The farmer had one sheep only! If he divided this sheep (which is best done by weight) into two parts, making one part two-thirds and the other part one-third, then the difference between these two numbers is the same as the difference between their squares – that is, one-third. Any two fractions will do if the denominator equals the sum of the two numerators.

# 9

## MRS HOBSON'S HEARTHRUG

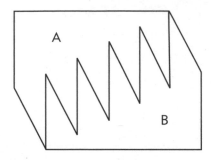

As the full measurements of the mutilated rug were given, it is quite an easy matter to find the precise dimensions for the square. The two pieces cut off would, if placed together, make an oblong piece 12 × 6, giving an area of 72, and as the original complete rug measured 36 × 27, it had an area of 972. If, therefore, we deduct the pieces that have been cut away, we find that our new rug will contain 972 less 72, or 900 ; and as 900 is the square of 30, we know that the new rug must measure 30 × 30 to be a perfect square. This is a great help towards the solution, because we may safely conclude that the two horizontal sides measuring 30 each may be left intact.

We can solve the puzzle by cutting the rug into just two pieces. It will be seen that if, after the cuts are made, we insert the teeth of the piece B one tooth lower down, the two portions will fit together and form a square.

# 10

## THE CHOCOLATE SQUARES

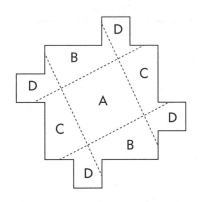

SQUARE A is left entire; the two pieces marked B fit together and make a second square; the two pieces C make a third square; and the four pieces marked D will form the fourth square.

# 11

## THE WIZARD'S CATS

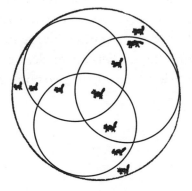

# 12

## THE THREE RAILWAY STATIONS

The three stations form a triangle, with sides 13, 14, and 15 miles. Make the 14 side the base; then the height of the triangle is 12 and the area 84. Multiply the three sides together and divide by four times the area. The result is eight miles and one-eighth, the distance required.

# 13

## FARMERS WURZEL'S ESTATE

The area of the complete estate is exactly 100 acres. To find this answer I use the following little formula $\dfrac{\sqrt{4ab - (a+b-)^2}}{4}$

where $a$, $b$, $c$ represent the three square areas, in any order. The expression gives the area of triangle A. This will be found to be 9 acres. It can be easily proved that A, B, C, and D are all equal in area; so the answer is 26 + 20 + 18 + 9 + 9 + 9 + 9 = 100 acres.

Here is the proof:

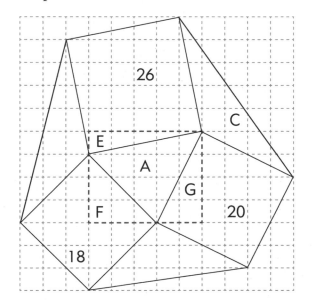

If every little dotted square in the diagram represents an acre, this must be a correct plan of the estate, for the squares of 5 and 1 together equal 26; the squares of 4 and 2 equal 20; and the squares of 3 and 3 added together equal 18. Now we see at once that the area of the triangle E is 2½, F is 4½, and G is 4. These added together make 11 acres, which we deduct from the area of the rectangle, 20 acres, and we find that the field A contains exactly 9 acres. If you want to prove that B, C, and D are equal in size to A, divide them in two by a line from the middle of the longest side to the opposite angle, and you will find that the two pieces in every case, if cut out, will exactly fit together and form A.

# 14

## THE CRESCENT PUZZLE

Referring to the original diagram, let A C be $x$, let C D be $x - 9$, and E C be $x - 5$. Then $x - 5$ is a mean proportional between $x - 9$ and $x$, from which we find that $x$ equals 25. Therefore the diameters are 50 inches and 41 inches respectively.

# 15

## THE DISSECTED CIRCLE

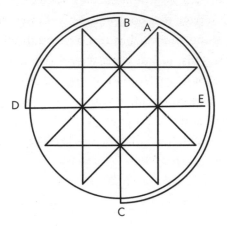

It can be done in twelve continuous strokes, thus: Start at A in the illustration, and eight strokes, forming the star, will bring you back to A; then one stroke round the circle to B, one stroke to C, one round the circle to D, and one final stroke to E – twelve in all. Of course, in practice the second circular stroke will be over the first one; it is separated in the diagram, and the points of the star not joined to the circle, to make the solution clear to the eye.

# 16

## THE INDUSTRIOUS BOOKWORM

The hasty reader will assume that the bookworm, in boring from the first to the last page of a book in three volumes, standing in their proper order on the shelves, has to go through all three volumes and four covers. This, in our case, would mean a distance of 9½ inches, which is a long way from the correct answer. You will find, on examining any three consecutive volumes on your shelves, that the first page of Vol. I and the last page of Vol. III are actually the pages that are nearest to Vol. II, so that the bookworm would only have to penetrate four covers (together, ½ inch) and the leaves in the second volume (3 inches) or a distance of 3½ inches, in order to tunnel from the first page to the last.

# 17

## THE CITY LUNCHEONS

The men may be grouped as follows, where each line represents a day and each column a table:

| | | | | | |
|----|----|----|----|----|----|
| AB | CD | EF | GH | IJ | KL |
| AE | DL | GK | FI | CB | HJ |
| AG | LJ | FH | KC | DE | IB |
| AF | JB | KI | HD | LG | CE |
| AK | BE | HC | IL | JF | DG |
| AH | EG | ID | CJ | BK | LF |
| AI | GF | CL | DB | EH | JK |
| AC | FK | DJ | LE | GI | BH |
| AD | KH | LB | JG | FC | EI |
| AL | HI | JE | BF | KD | GC |
| AJ | IC | BG | EK | HL | FD |

Note that in every column (except in the case of the As) all the letters descend cyclically in the same order, B, E, G, F, up to J, which is followed by B.

# 18

## THE WRONG HATS

The number of different ways in which eight persons, with eight hats, can each take the wrong hat is 14,833.

Here are the successive solutions for any number of persons from one to eight:

$$1 = 0$$
$$2 = 1$$
$$3 = 2$$
$$4 = 9$$
$$5 = 44$$
$$6 = 265$$
$$7 = 1,854$$
$$8 = 14,833$$

To get these numbers, multiply successively by 2, 3, 4, 5, etc. When the multiplier is even, add 1; when odd, deduct 1. Thus, $3 \times 1 - 1 = 2$; $4 \times 2 + 1 = 9$; $5 \times 9 - 1 = 44$; and so on. Or you can multiply the sum of the number of ways for $n - 1$ and $n - 2$ persons by $n - 1$, and so get the solution for $n$ persons. Thus, $4 (2 + 9) = 44$; $5 (9 + 44) = 265$; and so on.

# CHAPTER TEN

## CODEBREAKERS THROUGH THE LOOKING-GLASS

## 1

### THE CAPTIVE QUEEN

Since the baskets are of equal weight, we can assume that they exactly counterbalance each other halfway between the ground and the window. First, one of the baskets is pulled up to the window. The following table will indicate the order in which the family make their way to the ground. On some occasions, the weights in both baskets are equal, and it may be assumed that, by pulling on the ropes, it is possible to make the appropriate basket reach the ground.

*Key: Tower escape.*
Q = QUEEN. D = DAUGHTER. S = SON. W = WEIGHT.

| STEP | 0 | 1 | 2 | 3 | 4 | 5 | 6 | 7 | 8 | 9 |
|------|-----|-----|-----|-----|-----|-----|-----|-----|-----|-----|
| WINDOW LEVEL | QDS | QDW | QSW | QS | DSW | DS | DW | SW | S | W |
| GROUND LEVEL | W | S | D | DW | Q | QW | QS | QD | QDW | QDS |

264

# 2

## A GEOMETRICAL PARADOX

In the second 5 x 13 diagram, the diagonal is not a straight line, but is a slightly hollow quadrilateral with an area of one square.

# 3

## THE MONKEY AND WEIGHT PROBLEM

Lewis Carroll gave his own solution to the problem in a letter to Professor Price in which he states that, in his opinion, the 'weight' goes neither up nor down. However, the opinion of most mathematicians and scientists today is that the weight and monkey would always remain opposite to each other; hence, as the monkey climbs up the rope, the weight also goes up.

# 4.

## CROSSING THE RIVER

Code the four gentlemen and their wives as follows: Ml, Wl; M2, W2; M3, W3; M4 and W4. A possible solution is as follows:

| | |
|---|---|
| 1st crossing: | M1 and W1 cross; M1 returns |
| 2nd crossing: | M2 and W2 cross; M2 returns |
| 3rd crossing: | M1 and M2 cross; M2 and W2 return |
| 4th crossing: | W2 and W3 cross; M1 returns |
| 5th crossing: | M1 and M2 cross; W3 returns |
| 6th crossing: | M3 and M4 cross; M3 returns |
| 7th crossing: | M3 and W3 cross; M4 returns |
| 8th crossing: | M4 and W4 cross |

# 5

## DOUBLETS

| JOE | TILES | STALK | HOAX | JACK | DINNER |
|-----|-------|-------|------|------|--------|
| doe | tills | stale | coax | sack | sinner |
| die | tells | stare | coal | sick | singer |
| did | sells | scare | cool | silk | linger |
| aid | seals | score | FOOL | sill | longer |
| and | sears | scorn |      | JILL | conger |
| ANN | stars | ACORN |      |      | confer |
|     | stare |       |      |      | coffer |
|     | state |       |      |      | COFFEE |
|     | SLATE |       |      |      |        |

| BOAT | NOUN | SHIP | PLANT | UNIT | LIES |
|------|------|------|-------|------|------|
| bolt | noon | slip | plans | knit | lees |
| bold | moon | slap | plats | knot | fees |
| bald | morn | soap | peats | knob | feet |
| bard | more | soak | beats | snob | fret |
| bars | mere | sock | BEANS | snub | free |
| OARS | here | DOCK |       | snug | tree |
|      | herb |      |       | slug | TRUE |
|      | VERB |      |       | slur |      |
|      |      |      |       | sour |      |
|      |      |      |       | FOUR |      |

| HORSE | OPEN | CRY | BOWLER |
|-------|------|-----|--------|
| house | oven | coy | bowled |
| rouse | even | cot | cowled |
| route | eves | cut | cooled |
| routs | eyes | OUT | cooked |
| bouts | dyes |     | looked |
| boats | does |     | locked |
| brats | dots |     | licked |
| brass | dote |     | wicked |
| GRASS | date |     | WICKET |
|       | GATE |     |        |

# 6

## NAMES IN POEMS

The names are identified by the first letter in each line: LORINA, ALICE and EDITH.

The name is revealed by taking the second letter in each line: EDITH

# 7

## FEEDING THE CAT

That salmon and sole Puss should think very grand
    Is no remarkable thing.
For more of these dainties Puss took up her stand;
But when the third sister stretched out her fair hand
    Pray why should Puss swallow her ring?

# 8

## TWO TUMBLERS

Most people go for the first suggestion, since a spoonful of pure brandy was placed in the second tumbler, while only a mixture of brandy and water was taken back.

In fact, both suggestions are wrong. Since the tumblers were originally filled to the same level, they will again be equally full after the two transactions. The volume of brandy now missing from the first tumbler has been replaced by water from the second tumbler. Similarly, the amount of water missing from the second tumbler has been replaced by brandy from the first tumbler. The amount of brandy or water transferred is the same in each case.

# 9

## ELIGIBLE APARTMENTS

The day-room is number 9.

Let A be No. 9, B be No. 25, C be No. 52 and D be No. 73. By the theorem of Pythagoras, it will be determined that the distances between the rooms are as follows:

AB = 13, AC = 21, AD = 12+ (BETWEEN 12 AND 13)
BC = 20, BD = 21+, CD = 15+

Hence the sum of the distances from A is between 46 and 47; from B, between 54 and 55; from C, between 56 and 57; from D, between 48 and 51. Hence the sum is least for A.

# 10

## WHO'S COMING TO DINNER?

There is only one guest.

In this genealogy, males are denoted by capitals, and females by small letters. The Governor is E and his guest is C.

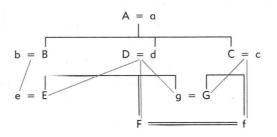

# CHAPTER ELEVEN

## GOOD, SMART, COMMON SENSE

## 1

### WHERE AM I?

You are at a railway station, as can be seen from the anagram answers below.

**a)** CAFÉ
**b)** CARRIAGE
**c)** PORTER
**d)** BARRIER
**e)** SUITCASE
**f)** TROLLEY
**g)** PLATFORM
**h)** TIMETABLE

## 2

### PICK UP STICKS

G, A, F, D, E, B, H, C

# 3

## CLOTHING COUPONS

**a)** TIE

**b)** CAPE

**c)** HAT

**d)** MITT

**e)** SUIT

**f)** VEST

**g)** FUR

**h)** BIB

# 4

## TON UP

*19 / 17 / 30 / 7 / 27*

# 5

## ODD ONE OUT

**a)** LUCIA – THE OTHERS ARE US STATES.

**b)** BLUNDER – THE OTHERS ARE FISH.

**c)** CIRCLE – THE OTHERS CAN BE FOLLOWED BY ROOT.

**d)** WINCHESTER – THE OTHERS ARE OXFORD COLLEGES.

**e)** CHICHESTER – THE OTHERS ARE CHEESES.

**f)** WOOL – THE OTHERS CAN HAVE A LETTER 'S' ADDED TO THE FRONT TO MAKE NEW WORDS.

# 6

## CREATURE CALCULATIONS

COBRA = 20. T = 1, A = 2, O = 3, R = 4, B = 5, C = 6

# 7

## LINK UP

ANTHEM, ASPIRE, BARROW, BETRAY, COTTON, DAMSON, EARTHY, FINALE, HUMOUR, LEGEND, METHOD, OFFICE, PALATE, PUPPET, WASHER.

# 8

## MANY HAPPY RETURNS

Ron is 42. His wife is 21. Steven is 21 and his wife is 22. Terry is 21 and his wife is 23.

# 9

## GOING TO THE PICTURES

### Grid A: BOB HOPE

**a)** DOUBTER

**b)** IGNORES

**c)** STABLED

**d)** REDHEAD

**e)** DEPOSIT

**f)** TORPEDO

**g)** GENERAL

### Grid B: (The Road to) MOROCCO

**a)** TERMINI

**b)** ACROBAT

**c)** ACTRESS

**d)** SCHOLAR

**e)** TOUCANS

**f)** TEACHER

**g)** INTONES

# 10
## ROTATION

Greater. The total of Y before rotation is 63 (3 + 19 + 30 + 11). The total of Y after five moves is 79 (6 + 24 + 33 + 16).

# 11
## MIDDLE DISTANCE

a) SHY, SLY

b) PULSE, PURSE

c) CONCERT, CONVERT

d) STUBBLE, STUMBLE

e) OUTCAST, OUTLAST

f) EXPANSE, EXPENSE

# 12
## VOWEL PLAY

a) Vowels removed completely. Message: WE NEED TO BE NEARER BEFORE WE ARE SAFE TO BE SEEN.

b) Each vowel is replaced by the next vowel in alphabetical order. So A becomes E, E becomes I, I becomes O, O becomes U and U becomes A. Message: WE ARE READY AND WAITING, ARE YOU?

c) Vowels swapped at random. Message: THE MORE WE ELABORATE OUR MEANS OF COMMUNICATION, THE LESS WE COMMUNICATE.

# 13
## POWER OF THREE

**a)** ALL

**b)** PIT

**c)** TOP

**d)** MEN

**e)** ROB

# 14
## DAYS

The total value of WET DAYS is 30. The name SUE has a total of 18. The values are: N = 9, W = 8, S = 7, U = 6, E = 5, T = 4, D = 3. The values of A and Y cannot be worked out, but between them they equal 3, i.e. they must be 1 and 2.

# 15
## DOUBLE COMBINATION

**a)** ONION

**b)** LEGIBLE

**c)** AMALGAM

**d)** THIRTIETH

**e)** STOCKIST

**f)** TEMPLATE

# 16

## SEEING IS BELIEVING

Number 1 appears twenty-one times. All the listed numbers appear when writing the numbers 1 to 100.

# 17

## ALL CHANGE

WHIST / WRIST / WREST / CREST / CRESS / CREWS
CLOCK / CLOAK / CROAK / CREAK / CREAM / DREAM

# 18

## SUM IT UP

**a)** The sum is 4451 + 3237 = 7688. The second column of digits from the left is the place to start: symbol + 2 = 6. No numbers are over 10, so the symbol must represent a 4. From then on there is only one combination of possibilities to make the sum work.

**b)** Take out the letters which can also be expressed as Roman numerals. FIVE contains IV, standing for four. EIGHT contains I, standing for one. SIX contains IX, standing for nine. SEVEN contains V, standing for five. NINE also contains I, standing for one. The sums are therefore as follows:

4 × 1 = 4
9 − 5 = 4
4 + 1 = 5

# 19

## WORD CHAIN

**a)** GROW, OWED, EDIT, ITCH, CHOP, OPEN, ENDS

**b)** CODE, DESK, SKID, IDEA, EAST, STEP, EPIC

**c)** ACHE, HEIR, IRON, ONLY, LYRE, REAP, APEX

**d)** KIWI, WIFE, FETE, TEAR, ARID, IDLE, LEAF

**e)** ZERO, ROSE, SEAL, ALTO, TOGA, GAME, MEND

# 20

## CIRCULAR TOUR

**a)** 33. Double each number then take away one to produce the next number. $17 \times 2 = 34$. Take away one to arrive at 33.

**b)** A for August. Sequence features the initial letters of months of the year.

**c)** 64. Each number is multiplied by itself and the answer written in the space that is opposite it. $2 \times 2 = 4$. $6 \times 6 = 36$. $8 \times 8 = 64$.

**d)** C. Then the circle reads anti-clockwise to spell out CONFUSED.

**e)** 243. Treble each number. $81 \times 3 = 243$.

**f)** YO. 'Happy Birthday to You' is the link. The first time the words appear as initial letters, then the second time the first two letters of each word appear.

# ACKNOWLEDGMENTS

First of all, grateful thanks to Sarah Armand, Gemma Briggs and Iain Standen at Bletchley Park; the work that has gone into restoring the codebreaking centre, and the huts in which those world-changing miracles took place, continues to draw in many thousands of visitors. For information on the Park, its many attractions and its opening hours, visit www.bletchleypark.org.uk.

Even more grateful thanks to the geniuses Roy and Sue Preston, who devise devious puzzles and problems with such style, flair and ingenuity. Huge thanks are also due to Radiya Hafiza, hawk-eyed copy-editor Lindsay Davies and particularly Grace Paul for the enormous job of bringing the book together with such speed, care and calm; also to Phoebe Swinburn, for letting the world know about it. And to Sarah Emsley, whose idea the book was in the first place!